ARIZONA FAV

Southwest Traditional to Light Modern Cooking

By Dorie F. Pass, R.D. and Dorothy Tegeler

Gem Guides Book Co.
315 Cloverleaf Dr., Suite F
Baldwin Park, CA 91706

Arizona Favorites
Copyright 1992
Dorothy Tegeler and Dorie F. Pass
Published by Gem Guides Book Co.

Special thanks to the following people for letting us use their recipes:

Laura Geisler	Cheese Enchiladas
Edwin Freed	Back East Fish Supreme
	Fresh Rhubarb Pie
Dixie Guss	Champagne Scallops
	Crab Enchiladas
Kent Stevens	Body Sculpture Burritos
Beth-Ann Kurtzman	Butterfield Brownies
Sarah Pass	Cowboy Cookies
Bill Doran	Arizona's Best Margaritas
Arizona's Finest Chefs	Restaurant Selections

Cover Design and Illustrations: Michael Stansbury

Published in the United States of America

Library of Congress Number 92-52501
ISBN 0-935182-55-1

For Larry, Paul and Laura

Contents

🍎 FOR YOUR COOKING CONVENIENCE 🍎

Arizona Favorite's has a new form of binding which allows it to lie flat. Simply press down on any open page and the book will remain in that position.

Introduction

We hope you'll enjoy selecting, preparing and eating the recipes you'll find in *Arizona Favorites* as much as we have enjoyed testing, tasting and writing this book.

Arizona is the youngest of the continental states. Complex societies thrived in Arizona more than a thousand years ago, long before the Europeans discovered the New World. The descendants of those early Native Americans still live in Arizona alongside the more recent Native American settlers and the new waves of immigrants from Mexico and the Snow and Rain Belts. You'll find the influence of Native Americans, Mexican Americans, Midwesterners, Northwesterners and Easterners in Arizona recipes.

From this melting pot of cultures we have chosen Arizona's best foods. The foods go beyond the usual tourist fare. These are the foods served in homes, at potlucks, at elegant cocktail parties, casual restaurants and in some of the world's finest resorts.

Arizona Foods

Where do Arizona foods fit in the spectrum of Southwestern cooking? You'll find they are generally milder than the fire-breathing dishes in New Mexican cuisine. Arizonans tend to prefer milder peppers, use a larger variety of ingredients and are not as heavily influenced by the barbecue-style sauces found in Tex-Mex dishes.

Local chefs have access to a bounty of fresh ingredients. Arizona is a leading producer of many fresh market vegetables and fruits such as lettuce, onions, broccoli, carrots, cauliflower, oranges, grapefruit, lemons, tangerines and grapes. Other specialty crops such as pecans, figs, dates and chile peppers also grow in the desert. When it's not in season here the nearby fertile California valleys supply the state. The Pacific coastal areas and Mexico's Baja Bay provide ready access to exceptional seafood.

All the recipes, except those provided by restaurants and resorts, have been author-tested, modified and simplified. We've kept in mind that most cooks, like us, are busy people who want delicious, simple to prepare foods. We have used ingredients that are generally available on your grocer's shelves, and which seldom require hours of preliminary preparation. If you have the time, you may find slight improvements in taste, or cost savings by beginning with a raw product such as dried beans instead of canned. Even good cooks, however, often start with a can of beans fresh from the grocer's shelf. And we know most busy cooks do.

These are the foods we eat. Even with shelves of cookbooks, we reach for these recipes first. Each revision of the manuscript bears food splatters as testimony to our enjoyment of these foods.

We have tried to provide variety in the recipes. While there are many seasonings and ingredients that are frequently found in Southwestern dishes, Arizona food, unlike some other regional foods, does not all taste the same.

Nutritional Options

We offer lower calorie and lower fat options wherever possible. You should keep in mind that the substitutions may influence the final taste. The best way to reduce calories is to simply consume smaller portions. We relied on seasonings other than salt where possible to provide the flavors.

You will find nutritional information listed below selected recipes. The number of calories, amount of protein, carbohydrates, fat, cholesterol, sodium and fiber per serving are listed in the following format.

Cal	Pro	Carb	Fat	Chol	Sod	Fib

These recipes reflect lower calorie and lower fat content.

The American Heart Association along with the American Dietetic Association recommend limiting fat content to thirty percent of our daily intake. A high fat diet has been associated with the development of heart disease and several other disease states, including several forms of cancer and obesity.

Fat is the most caloric source of calories, containing nine calories per gram. To determine the recommended number of fat grams in your own diet begin with your daily calorie intake. Find thirty percent of that number. This will determine the number of calories that can be consumed from fat. Next convert calories to fat grams by dividing by 9. The following example makes this easier to understand.

If your diet contains 1500 total calories per day, multiply 1500 x .30 which gives you 450 calories. Then divide 450 by 9. The result is 50 grams of fat allowed per day.

If you are unsure of the total number of calories that you require you may want to meet with a Registered Dietitian for a nutrition consultation. You may also write down everything you consume and the quantity for a typical day. Then using a reliable calorie counting reference book find the calorie value for each food. This will give you a ballpark figure of your total daily calories from which to begin calculating your recommended grams of fat per day.

We have tried to be conscientious with all of our recipes to provide the highest consistency in flavor, in quality, and a low-fat cooking style, but due to the nature of Southwest cooking, as with other regional foods, it is sometimes impossible to get the desired end product without indulging slightly with traditional ingredients.

It is possible to adjust these recipes by substituting low-fat products, for example, low-fat or non-fat milk, low-fat sour cream, plain low-fat yogurt, reduced calorie or fat-free mayonnaise. These products will enable you to make choices which will further reduce the fat and calories to meet your dietary needs.

We have given approximate preparation times and serving sizes to help you estimate how much to prepare. Preparation times listed include cooking time.

Special thanks go to taste testers, Larry, Paul and Laura, who have shared this adventure with us and have been exceptionally supportive. An assortment of relatives and friends who have dropped by on cooking day to taste also deserve thanks. They've been a constant reminder to us that some like it hot and some like it mild. Some like it sweet and some like it zesty. They've each found their own favorites among this collection. We're delighted that we could include special recipes from various friends and relatives.

Restaurant Selections

We are also indebted to all of the Arizona chefs and cooks from the restaurants and resorts who shared a bit of their own culinary arts and kindly let us have a glimpse of how they prepare these marvelous dishes. They've given us new respect for their skills in complex procedures that often seem to have been effortless when the final dish is presented. Among this collection there's something that will appeal to everyone, regardless of whether you consider yourself an ultra-sophisticated gourmet, or if you prefer simpler fare. These recipes are highlighted as a "Restaurant Selection."

So whether it is a bowl of Bob Brock's famous Tortilla Flat Killer Chili or Chef Christopher Gross' renowned Chocolate Tower, you'll find foods you'll love here. Some of you will want to rush to your own kitchen to see if you can get the same fantastic results. Others may put a particular restaurant on their dining-out itinerary. And if you're like us, you may find that it is simply fun to read how much creativity, planning and care goes into the preparation of these foods. We have gained a new appreciation for the wizardry that is performed in restaurant kitchens.

Now to get started. The best approach to any cooking project is good organization. So make a pitcher of margaritas, sit back and raise your feet, then begin selecting recipes.

Arizona's Best Margaritas

Our friend Bill Doran loaned us his favorite margarita recipe. He's especially fond of them when he returns to land after a day fishing in the Baja Bay down Mexico way.

6 oz. tequila
2 oz. cointreau
1 oz. triple sec
2 C. margarita mix
ice cubes to fill blender

Combine all ingredients in a blender. Blend until ice is slushy. Dip glass rims in salt. Fill with margaritas and serve with lime slices.

Serves: 4
Preparation Time: 5 minutes

Arizona Seasonings

Cayenne pepper: Always used ground, cayenne is derived from the very hot red capsicum peppers. Use sparingly.

Chili powder: A blend of cumin, oregano, garlic powder, salt, allspice and coriander.

Chili sauce: A thick, catsup-like sauce containing bits of garlic, onions and corn syrup.

Cilantro: Sometimes called Chinese parsley, cilantro is commonly available dried. It can usually be found fresh in the produce department or in Oriental food markets. Cilantro is also frequently used in Hungarian cooking. It is often used fresh in salads and salsas. When used in cooked foods, add near the end of the preparation.

Coriander: The seed of the cilantro, coriander has a milder flavor than its leafy sibling and is often used in main dishes and desserts.

Crushed red pepper: A dried, hot red pepper that has been crushed. It includes the seeds and is very hot.

Cumin: An ancient spice, it is most often used ground, although some recipes may call for whole seeds. Cumin has a powerful and distinct taste. Use sparingly, an eighth of a teaspoon is noticeable.

Epazote: A subtle-flavored herb often added in small quantities to bean dishes to reduce flatulence and aid in digestion. It is sometimes called pazote or Jerusalem oak. It can be omitted without changing the flavor of the recipe.

Garlic: An aromatic herb which grows in bulbs and separates into cloves. Garlic has traditionally been considered a medicinal herb. It is generally crushed with the flat blade of the knife before chopping or minced through a garlic press. There is no substitute for the unforgettable aromatic qualities of garlic. Garlic powder is more concentrated than fresh garlic. A quarter or an eighth of a teaspoon is usually enough.

Hot pepper sauce: A liquid form of chiles made by combining the pulp of hot chiles with vinegar and salt. Use it as a table condiment when you are serving a crowd whose tolerance for heat varies. Hot pepper sauce is frequently sold under the name Tobasco.™

Onions: A member of the lily family, this herb is a staple in Arizona cooking. Unless specified otherwise, yellow or Bermuda onions are preferred for most dishes.

Oregano: From the mint family, oregano is one of the most commonly used spices in Mexican cooking and is very similar to marjoram. Also, oregano is used frequently in Italian and Chinese cooking.

Salsa: Fresh or canned tomatoes, onions, peppers and other seasonings. Sometimes called picante sauce. Served with tortilla chips as an appetizer or as a topping for many salads and entrées.

Taco sauce: A thin, tomato-based sauce containing chili peppers and seasonings.

Chile Peppers

If you are new to Southwestern cooking, you'll soon learn that there's definitely a difference in the heat and taste among varieties of chile peppers. You'll discover that as your taste for peppers matures you'll gradually be ready to progress to the use of hotter peppers. Green and red bell peppers are the mildest with almost no heat and a sweet flavor. From there it is an easy step to the Mexi-Bells and Anaheims. Begin by adding small amounts, taste testing and then adding more. It's much easier to add more than to remove too many. The intensity of peppers is known to vary within the variety and even between peppers grown on the same plant.

You can test the heat of the chile by rubbing your finger across the outer skin and then licking your finger. But be very careful with the hotter varieties. Do not touch your face, eyes or any other sensitive areas before washing your hands thoroughly with soap and water. Rubber gloves will protect your hands when preparing the hotter varieties of peppers.

Most recipes call for the skin to be removed before using the chile. The simplest way we've found is to clean the chile with water. Place it whole on a hot barbecue grill and allow the outer skin to blacken. Remove and place in a plastic bag for five minutes. The outer skin will lift away easily at this point. For a milder taste discard the seeds. If you don't have access to a grill, place the chile under a broiler until the skin blisters. Then follow the same procedure as for grill preparation.

If you have a sensitive mouth and find your tongue sizzling, try a spoonful of sugar to neutralize the discomfort.

Anaheim: Also known as California or Green chiles, they are usually about four to six inches long and are available fresh or canned at the grocery store. The canned varieties are usually labeled as "Green Chiles." They are available in varying heats. When left to ripen in the fields they turn red and are used in making red chile powder.

Ancho: The dried poblano chile is the most commonly used dried chile. About three to five inches long, it is a deep-brownish red.

Banana: Also called Hungarian Wax, Yellow Hots or Guero, banana peppers are pale yellow, long and tapered. It's not necessary to remove the thin skin before using.

11

Bell: Traditionally green or red, you'll now find golden, purple, orange and white varieties. This pepper has almost no heat. Green bells are usually the least expensive and are less sweet.

Habanero: The world's hottest.

Jalapeño: These are small very hot chiles. They are dark green, fat and about three inches long. Jalapeños are available fresh, canned or pickled.

Mexi-Bell: Similar to bell peppers, with just a slight kick.

Poblano: The fresh form of the ancho chile, the poblano is usually mild and similar in size and flavor to bell peppers.

Serrano: These are small, but even hotter than jalapeños.

Beans

With more than fifty varieties of beans available it's no wonder that a new generation is discovering the nutritional value of beans. High in protein, minerals and cholesterol-reducing fiber, beans are also low in sodium and contain no cholesterol. Arizona cooking offers a number of great ways to prepare beans in tasty ways. If you're trying to acquire a taste for beans we recommend two recipes in particular, the Pollo Rancho and the Roaring Springs Bean Soup. Even non-bean lovers will like these.

The recipes in this book call for canned beans in the interest of easy preparation. But dried beans can easily be substituted. Dried beans, prepared fresh, have a much lower sodium content than canned beans.

To prepare dried beans rinse thoroughly before cooking and remove any discolored beans. Soak in cold water for 8 hours. Discard the water used to soak the beans and rinse well. Don't overlook this step, since sugars accumulate in the water and can make digestion more difficult. To cook, cover with three parts fresh water to one part beans. Bring to a boil and cook for 10 minutes. Lower heat to simmer and cook covered for another 1-1/2 to 2 hours until beans are tender, but not mushy. 2 cups of dry beans will yield 5-6 cups of cooked beans.

Black beans: Small black, kidney-shaped beans. Mild and sweet, they have a full earthy flavor and are excellent mashed, refried or in salads.

Great Northern beans: White beans a little less than one-half inch long and oval-shaped. They are the mature dried seeds of green string beans with a mild flavor, especially good in casseroles.

Kidney beans: The basic chile bean. Kidney beans are usually a deep red to brown and are about a half inch long.

Pinto beans: Smaller than a kidney bean, yet larger than a black bean, these pinkish-beige beans have a mild flavor.

Garbanzo beans: Also called chick peas, these ball-shaped tan beans are often eaten cold in salads.

Refried beans: Mashed pinto beans seasoned with onion, garlic and tomato. When buying already processed, choose vegetarian style, and check the ingredients to be sure they contain no lard.

Specialty Foods Frequently Used in Arizona Cooking

Jicama: This is a potato-like vegetable with a rough brown skin and crisp sweet white flesh. It is most frequently used in salads. Take care when peeling the tough skin. Jicama is usually available fresh in the produce department. Slice and soak in lime juice for an easy appetizer.

Tomatillos: These are small green tomatoes with a thin, dry husk. They are usually available fresh or canned and are the basic ingredient in many green sauces. These Mexican green tomatoes have a flavor which is quite different from tomatoes grown in the U.S. Do not substitute the immature fruit of a red tomato for a tomatillo.

Tomatoes: Commonly found in many Arizona dishes and used as a garnish for others. If the recipe calls for peeled tomatoes, plunge in boiling water for 30 seconds then rinse with cold water. The skins will slip off easily.

Tortillas: Flat rounds made from ground corn or wheat flour. While they can be made from the raw ingredients, your grocer generally carries several styles that are quite acceptable and ready to use. Check the label to be sure the brand you select has not been prepared with lard. They can be warmed quickly by placing in a plastic bag and heating in the microwave. There are endless ways of using a tortilla. Among them:

> **burrito:** large flour tortilla, with a filling
> **chimichanga:** fried meat-filled burrito
> **nachos:** tortilla chips, often topped with melted cheese and peppers
> **enchilada:** rolled tortilla with filling and sauce
> **tostada:** a flat fried tortilla topped with assorted fillings

Tamales: Corn-based bread, corn husks filled with meats or sweets and steamed.

Pinon nuts: Also called pine nuts. These are found wild in parts of the Southwest. They are found on pine cones. In other areas they can be purchased at health food stores, specialty food shops or in the gourmet section of your local market.

Spanish for Gringos

Here is a handy guide to a few words that are used in the recipes which have Spanish origins.

albondigas	meatball soup
carne	meat
cerveza	beer
churro	fried dessert
Cinco de Mayo	Fifth of May
frijoles	beans
gazpacho	cold tomato soup
guacamole	avocado dip
huevos	eggs
molinos	mills
pescado	fish
pollo	chicken
puerco	pork
relleno	filled pepper
rojo	red
salsa	sauce
sopa	soup
sopaipilla	dessert
verde	green

APPETIZERS, DIPS AND SAUCES

If onion soup mix and sour cream is the only thing that ever pops into your mind when it's time to prepare a dip, get ready for some compliments. This assortment of appetizers, dips and sauces will be a wonderful change of pace. From hot and spicy to cool and creamy, we have an appetizer for all occasions -- and now you will, too!

When you're in the mood for traditional, authentic Arizona favorites, try the Thick and Chunky Salsa, Guacamole or Bean Dip. For an out-of-the-ordinary way to enjoy cholesterol-free eggs, try our Devil's Hole Deviled Eggs. And if you're looking for that special flair for an up-and-coming cocktail party, you couldn't do better than The Boulders Lobster Corn Fritters.

Guacamole

Cabelleros Bean Dip

Taco Dip

Blue Corn Chip Dip

Gold Rush Pecan Spread

Thick and Chunky Salsa

Tortilla Flat's Salsa

Black Bean Salsa

Devil's Hole Deviled Eggs

The Boulders Lobster Corn Fritters

Bean Roundups

Hearts of Palm

Creamy Crab Swirls

Los Abrigados Fried Avocados

Guacamole

Arizona-style cooking is never complete without a dollop of sour cream and a mound of guacamole. Guacamole goes well with chips, on a chimichanga or as a topping for taco salad.

2 avocados, peeled and mashed
1 med. onion, chopped
2 cloves garlic, minced
1 lg. tomato, peeled and chopped
8 oz. sour cream
1 T. lemon juice
1/2 tsp. salt
dash of pepper
dash of coriander

Combine all ingredients until blended well. Chill and serve.

Serves: 15
Preparation Time: 15 minutes

Cabelleros Bean Dip

A traditional Southwestern favorite. You can turn up the heat by switching to a hotter chili (jalapeño or serrano) or by adding more hot sauce.

1 (15-1/2-oz.) can pinto beans, drained and rinsed
3 T. cream cheese (or light cream cheese)
2 green onions (scallions), chopped fine
1 (4-oz.) can green chiles, diced
1 T. taco sauce
3 drops hot sauce

In a small bowl, mash pinto beans with a fork. Add all other ingredients and blend well. Chill a few hours to allow flavors to blend. Bring to room temperature and serve with chips.

Serves: 8
Preparation Time: 15 minutes

Cal	Pro	Carb	Fat	Chol	Sod	Fib
107	5g	17g	2g	6mg	47mg	5g

Taco Dip

Dip your chips into this medley of ingredients. Our friends and guests never seem to be able to get enough.

8 oz. sour cream (or light sour cream)
8 oz. cream cheese, softened (or light cream cheese)
1 ripe avocado, peeled and mashed
1 T. seasoning salt
2 C. iceberg lettuce, chopped
1 green pepper, chopped
1 lg. tomato, chopped
1 C. mozzarella cheese, grated
1 C. cheddar cheese, grated
1/2 C. black olives, sliced (optional)
3 green onions (scallions), sliced (optional)

In a medium bowl, mix together sour cream, cream cheese, avocado and seasoning salt. Spread on a large flat tray. Layer remaining ingredients on top of the cheese-avocado mixture. Chill and serve with tortilla chips.

Serves 12
Preparation Time: 20 minutes

Blue Corn Chip Dip

This creamy vegetable dip has so much zest that it will make you sit up and take notice. The taste and color complement the blue corn chips.

1 (4-oz.) can green chiles, diced and drained
1 green onion (scallion), cut in 1-inch pieces
1/2 C. red pepper, seeded and cut into pieces
2 cloves garlic
6 oz. sour cream (or light sour cream)
blue corn chips

Place all ingredients except sour cream and chips in the food processor. Blend until pureed. Pour the mixture into a small bowl. Add sour cream and combine well. Refrigerate for several hours or overnight. Serve with blue corn chips.

Serves 10 to 12
Preparation Time: 15 minutes

Gold Rush Pecan Spread

A different and delicious spread that's sure to get out-of-the-ordinary compliments.

2 eggs, hard cooked
2 oz. pecans
1 C. cheddar cheese, grated
1/2 C. green onion (scallions), cut in 1-inch pieces
3 T. chili sauce

In the bowl of an electric food processor, combine all ingredients and process until smooth. Serve with crackers.

Serves 10 to 12
Preparation Time: 25 minutes

Thick and Chunky Salsa

All you need are the chips. You'll never open another jar again.

3 lg. tomatoes, skinned, seeded and chopped
1 med. onion, chopped
1 clove garlic, minced
1 (16-oz.) can tomato sauce
1 Anaheim chili, skinned, seeded and diced
1 T. fresh cilantro, minced

In the bowl of a food processor, combine all ingredients. Blend until chunky. Do not overprocess. Serve with chips, or as an entrée topping.

Serves 8 to 10
Preparation Time: 20 minutes

Cal	Pro	Carb	Fat	Chol	Sod	Fib
27	1g	6g	0g	0mg	294mg	1g

RESTAURANT SELECTION

Salsa

Tortilla Flat
Tortilla Flat, AZ

2 hot yellow peppers
2 jalapeños
2 long green chiles
1 lg. onion (or 2 small)
1/2 to 1 bunch cilantro
1 (6-lb.) can crushed tomatoes
1/4 oz. cumin
1/2 oz. salt
1/2 oz. garlic powder
tortilla chips for dipping

Finely chop peppers, onion and cilantro. Add to crushed tomatoes. Add spices. Stir. Let sit overnight in the fridge. Serve with tortilla chips or your favorite recipe.

Serves 35

Black Bean Salsa

A tasty chip dip or an innovative topping for a burro.

1 (15-1/2-oz.) can black beans
1/3 C. prepared salsa
3 drops hot sauce
1/4 C. chives, chopped

In a small bowl, combine first three ingredients. Sprinkle with chives. Refrigerate until ready to serve.

Serves 10
Preparation Time: 5 minutes

Devil's Hole Deviled Eggs

If deviled eggs have always been one of your picnic favorites, this no-cholesterol version is one you can enjoy guilt-free. When you're not in the mood for eggs, the filling makes a terrific dip.

10 hard cooked eggs

Filling
1 (8-oz.) can vegetarian-style refried beans
1/4 C. green pepper, chopped fine
1 T. chili sauce

Cut eggs in half. Remove and discard yolks. In a small bowl, blend together filling ingredients. Microwave on high for 1-1/2 minutes. Transfer the bean mixture into a pastry bag fitted with a large nozzle. Fill egg center. Serve warm or at room temperature. Yields 20 halves.

Serves 10
Preparation Time: 30 minutes

Cal	Pro	Carb	Fat	Chol	Sod	Fib
32	2g	5g	1g	0	29mg	2g

RESTAURANT SELECTION

Lobster Corn Fritters

The Boulders
34361 N. Darlington Drive
Carefree

With incredible boulder-strewn views and exceptional food, it's certainly worth the drive to sample the fare at this premiere resort.

2 ears sweet corn, steamed for 5 minutes
1 T. olive oil
4 scallions
1 clove garlic, minced
3/4 C. flour
1 C. milk
1/2 tsp. kosher salt
pinch of freshly ground pepper
2 egg whites
1 lobster (about 2 lbs.) cooked, shelled and cut into pieces

Cut corn kernels off cob into a stainless bowl. Heat the oil and sauté scallions and garlic; add to corn. Add flour and stir to coat. Add milk, salt and pepper and mix well. (Mixture should be pasty, about 80% corn and 20% batter.)

Whisk egg whites with a pinch of salt until medium stiff peaks form; fold into batter. Place pieces of lobster, red side down, on a medium hot oiled griddle about 4 inches apart. Drop approximately 1-1/2 tablespoons of the batter over the lobster and cook a minute or two. Flip and cook other side. Serve lobster side up. Yields 20 fritters.

Serves 10

Chef Charles Wiley

Bean Roundups

These appetizers always prove to be favorites. They'll take the edge off hunger in mid-afternoon or at the pre-dinner cocktail party.

1 (16-oz.) can vegetarian-style refried beans
1/4 C. onion, chopped
1/2 tsp. hot sauce
2 C. prepared baking mix
1 C. sour cream or plain low-fat yogurt
1 (4-oz.) can green chiles, diced
1 C. Monterey Jack cheese, grated

Preheat oven to 400°F. In a small bowl, combine beans, onion and hot sauce. In a large bowl, combine baking mix and sour cream. Mix until sour cream is well-incorporated. If dough appears sticky, add another 1/4 cup of baking mix.

Knead on a floured board for 2 minutes. Roll out into a 1/4-inch thick rectangle. Using a 2-inch round cookie cutter, cut out circles and place on an ungreased cookie sheet. On each circle, place (in layers) 1-1/2 teaspoons bean mixture, a pinch of green chiles and 1 teaspoon cheese. Bake for 15 to 18 minutes, until golden brown. Yields 30 round-ups.

Serves: 15
Preparation Time: 40 minutes

Hearts of Palm

If you're looking for a tasty way to please the vegetarians in your life, this may be it.

1 T. butter
1 T. flour
dash of pepper
1/2 C. milk
1 (6-oz.) jar marinated hearts of palm, drained and chopped
2 T. fresh parsley, chopped
1/2 tsp. garlic powder
1/2 tsp. onion powder
pastry for a 2-crust pie
dash of paprika

Preheat oven to 375°F. Spray a cookie sheet with non-stick vegetable oil. In a small saucepan, melt butter, stir in flour and pepper. Add milk and cook until thickened. Remove from heat. Add hearts of palm, parsley, garlic and onion powder. Combine well and set aside.

On a floured surface, roll out pastry until it is 1/16-inch thick. With a cookie cutter, cut out 4-inch circles. Spoon a generous tablespoon of the palm mixture into the center of each circle. Fold over. Crimp the edges with a fork. Sprinkle the top with paprika. Bake for 25 minutes. Serve with salsa. Yields 24 appetizers.

Serves: 12
Preparation Time: 60 minutes

Creamy Crab Swirls

The colorful presentation of this dainty appetizer will tantalize your guests as well as your taste buds.

1/2 lb. fresh or imitation crab
2 T. shredded coconut
1 tsp. dried red chili pepper flakes
3 T. red pepper, minced
3 cucumbers, cut in half and cored

In a medium bowl, mix together all ingredients except the cucumber. Peel the cucumber. Cut vertically in half and hollow out seeds. Cucumber will look like two tubes. Stuff with the crab mixture. Slice in 1/4-inch sections. Yields 45 crab swirls.

Serves: 15
Preparation Time: 15 minutes

Fried Avocados

Los Abrigados
Canyon Rose
Sedona

1 bottle Mexican beer
3 C. flour
1/2 C. cilantro, chopped
salt and cayenne pepper to taste
sprinkling of flour
2 avocados, cut in quarters
prickly pear cactus jelly or barbecue sauce

Coat: Pour the beer into a mixing bowl. Add flour gradually until the mixture has the consistency of thick pancake batter. Mix in the cilantro, salt and cayenne pepper. Sprinkle flour on a plate. Dip the avocados in the flour, and then in the beer batter.

Deep fry 3 minutes: Fry the avocados in oil until they are crispy. When done, place them on paper towels to absorb the grease.

Serve: Serve with prickly pear cactus jelly or barbecue sauce.

Serves: 2

Executive Chef Todd Hall

SOUPS

We don't generally boast about how great our recipes are, but when it comes to soups we think you'll forgive us for telling you this is one of the best collections of soup recipes you'll find anywhere. They're simply delicious and most can be prepared in less than one hour.

For a traditional favorite try the Mexican Chicken Soup. For a true Arizona taste treat the Cream of Green Chile Soup will be a pleasant surprise. We've gotten compliments galore on our Roaring Springs Bean Soup, which is not only nutritious, but also delicious.

We've found that most cooks have their own special way of preparing broth, and since many of our recipes call for the addition of broth, you can use fresh, canned or bouillon cubes or granules dissolved in hot water. For fresh broth, use the water in which meat or vegetables have been cooked. If you are using bouillon, follow the manufacturer's directions, unless one of our recipes specifically calls for a certain number of bouillon cubes, and a certain amount of water.

Roaring Springs Bean Soup

Southwestern Onion Soup

Albondigas

Los Abrigados Billy Bi Mussel and Saffron Soup

Pumpkin and Shrimp Soup

Cream of Corn Soup

Chicken and Corn Soup

Arizona Kitchen's Wigwam Smoked Corn Chowder

Mexican Chicken Soup

The Tack Room's Tortilla Soup from Yucatan, Mexico

Cream of Green Chili Soup

Icebox Gazpacho

Cream of Gazpacho

Plain Ole Chili

Vegetarian Chili

Tortilla Flat's Killer Chili

Apricot Fruit Compote

Roaring Springs Bean Soup

Prepare this as a first course or as the main dish. It's a hearty tomato-based soup that is truly delicious.

1 lg. onion, chopped
2 cloves garlic, minced
1 T. vegetable oil
2-1/2 C. water
1 C. chicken broth
1 (15-oz.) can tomato puree
1 (15-1/2-oz.) can kidney beans, drained and rinsed
1 (15-1/2-oz.) can garbanzo beans, drained and rinsed
2 C. cooked brown rice
1 green pepper, chopped
6 oz. raw spinach, cleaned and trimmed
1 tsp. basil
1 tsp. Mexican oregano leaves

In a large saucepan, sauté onion and garlic in oil until transparent. Add remaining ingredients. Bring to a boil, then reduce heat and cover. Simmer for 20 minutes.

Serves: 9
Preparation Time: 40 minutes

Cal	Pro	Carb	Fat	Cho	Sod	Fib
210	10g	38g	3g	0mg	440mg	9g

Southwestern Onion Soup

This brothy-style flavorful soup is a good way to start any meal.

1 (15-1/2-oz.) can pinto beans, drained and rinsed
1 (15-1/2-oz.) can kidney beans, drained and rinsed
1 qt. water
2 lg. bay leaves
6 black peppercorns
1 lg. onion, chopped finely
1 lg. onion, cut into rings
1 tsp. chili powder
1 T. tomato paste
1 T. dried parsley
1 tsp. salt

In a large saucepan, combine all ingredients. Bring to a boil, cover and simmer for 45 minutes. Discard bay leaves and serve.

Serves: 4 to 6
Preparation Time: 1 hour

Cal	Pro	Carb	Fat	Cho	Sod	Fib
222	13g	42g	1g	0mg	438mg	16g

Albondigas

Not quite a soup, not quite a stew. Flavorful, but not overbearing, Albondigas is a traditional Mexican meatball soup.

1 med. onion, chopped
1 clove garlic, minced
1 T. vegetable oil
2 C. beef broth
2 C. water
1 (6-oz.) can tomato paste
2 med. potatoes, peeled and cubed
2 med. carrots, peeled and sliced
1 egg, beaten
1/4 C. fresh parsley, chopped
1/2 tsp. dried cilantro
1/2 tsp. Mexican oregano leaves
dash of pepper
1 lb. ground beef, lean
1/4 C. white rice

In a large saucepan, sauté onion and garlic in oil until transparent. Stir in beef broth, water and tomato paste and bring to a boil. Add potatoes and carrots and reduce heat to simmer.

In a medium bowl, blend egg, parsley, cilantro, oregano and pepper. Add ground beef and rice. Mix well. Shape meat into 1-inch balls. Drop meatballs a few at a time into the soup. Bring to a boil, cover and reduce to a simmer for 30 minutes.

Serves: 8
Preparation Time: 50 minutes

Billy Bi
Mussel and Saffron Soup

Los Abrigados
Canyon Rose
Sedona

5 lbs. fresh black mussels, in shell
2 qts. heavy cream
1 large pinch saffron
4 celery stalks, chopped
4 carrots
1 bay leaf
1 bunch thyme
kosher salt and fresh ground black pepper to taste

Place all ingredients in soup pot. Cook for 2 hours at a simmer. Strain and serve.

Serves: 6 to 8

Executive Chef Todd Hall

Pumpkin and Shrimp Soup

From Halloween to Thanksgiving our thoughts often turn to pumpkin. Here's a nifty way to use this autumn fruit in an easy-to-make and satisfying soup.

1 onion, chopped
2 stalks celery, chopped
1 tsp. vegetable oil
1 (8-oz.) can pumpkin
1 lb. raw shrimp, peeled and deveined
2 C. 2% low-fat milk
3 C. chicken broth
2 C. cooked white rice
dash of nutmeg
salt and pepper to taste

In a large saucepan, sauté onion and celery in oil until transparent. Add remaining ingredients. Heat thoroughly for approximately 15 minutes and serve.

Serves: 8
Preparation Time: 30 minutes

Cal	Pro	Carb	Fat	Chol.	Sod	Fib
181	19g	20g	3g	81mg	571mg	3g

Cream of Corn Soup

This hearty soup makes a great choice for a soup and sandwich luncheon.

1/4 C. butter or margarine
1 small onion, diced
2 T. flour
2 C. 2% low-fat milk
1 C. chicken broth
1 (4-oz.) can green chiles, diced
1 (16-oz.) pkg. frozen corn
salt and pepper to taste
1/2 C. cheddar cheese, grated

In a medium saucepan, sauté onion in butter until transparent. Add flour and stir until mixture thickens. Add milk and continue stirring. The soup will thicken as it cooks. Add chicken broth, chiles, corn, salt and pepper and stir until heated. Top with cheese and serve.

Serves: 6
Preparation Time: 30 minutes

Chicken and Corn Soup

As this soup simmers, the kitchen will fill with a mouth-watering aroma and you'll have a steady stream of inquiries as to what's cooking.

1 (3-lb.) chicken, cut into pieces, with skin removed
1 onion, peeled and cut into chunks
2 stalks celery (including tops), cut into 1-inch pieces
3 lg. carrots, peeled and cut into 1-inch pieces
1 bunch fresh parsley (stems removed)
1/2 tsp. black peppercorns
6 C. water
6 ears fresh corn, husked
2 T. chili sauce

In an 8-quart stock pan, combine all ingredients except corn and chili sauce and cook over high heat until water boils. Reduce heat to medium, cover and simmer for 1 hour.

Remove from heat. Using a colander, drain chicken and vegetables reserving the broth. Discard vegetables except for the carrots. Remove chicken from the bone and break into bite-size pieces. Set aside along with the carrots. Holding corn ears vertically on a flat board, slice kernels from the cob, using a large knife with a downward stroke.

Return broth to saucepan and add corn. Cook over medium heat for 10 minutes. Add chicken and carrots and stir in chili sauce. Serve hot.

Serves: 6 to 8
Preparation Time: 1-1/2 hours

Cal	Pro	Carb	Fat	Chol	Sod	Fib
244	17g	31g	4g	36mg	125mg	4g

Wigwam Smoked Corn Chowder

Arizona Kitchen
The Wigwam Resort
Litchfield Park

More than sixty years old, The Wigwam Resort has received the Mobil Five Star rating for sixteen consecutive years. A $45 million renovation project was completed in the early 1990s.

4 ears corn on the cob
1/4 C. butter
1/4 C. onion
1/4 C. celery
1/4 C. leeks
1/8 C. carrots
1/4 C. red bell pepper
1/4 C. green bell pepper
1/4 C. red or baker potatoes
2 cloves garlic
1 T. thyme
1 bay leaf
1/2 tsp. cinnamon
6 C. chicken stock
8 oz. roux (4 oz. butter and 4 oz. flour)
1 C. cream style corn
1 qt. heavy cream
salt and white pepper to taste

Clean ears of corn. Place in smoker and smoke for 20 minutes or until dark brown. Remove kernels from ears, set aside. Heat a Dutch oven. When hot, add butter and melt. Sauté vegetables, including garlic but excluding corn, along with thyme, bay leaf and cinnamon. While vegetables are sautéeing, bring chicken stock to a boil. Whip in roux, small amounts at a time. Whipping constantly until the liquid boils, then turn down heat and simmer 20 minutes. Strain the sauce through a china cap into the sautéed vegetables.

Stir in cream style corn and allow to simmer 5 minutes. Check by taste, if potatoes are cooked throughout. Add smoked corn kernels. Heat heavy cream. Bring to a boil and reduce by half, then add to the chowder. Give soup a final stir and season with salt and white pepper to taste. Yields 1 gallon.

Serves: 16
Chef Michael Garbin

Mexican Chicken Soup

Nearly every ethnic culture has its own version of chicken soup. This is a truly Mexican-style blend. Colorful and nutritious, it'll soon become a family favorite.

1(3-lb.) chicken, cut into pieces with skin removed
1 med. onion, sliced
3 stalks celery (including tops) cut into 1-inch pieces
1 bunch fresh parsley (stems removed)
1/8 tsp. black pepper
6 C. water
1 (14-1/2-oz.) can tomatoes, cut up
3 carrots, sliced
1 med. onion, chopped
1 zucchini, sliced
1 C. frozen peas

In a large saucepan, combine chicken, onion, celery, parsley, pepper and water. Bring to a boil. Cover and simmer for 1-1/2 hours. Using a colander, drain chicken and vegetables reserving the broth. Discard the vegetables.

Remove chicken from the bone and cube. Return chicken and broth to the saucepan. Add tomatoes, carrots and onions. Cover and simmer for 30 minutes. Add zucchini and peas and cook an additional 10 minutes.

Serves: 8
Preparation Time: 2-1/2 hours

Cal	Pro	Carb	Fat	Chol	Sod	Fib
118	13g	10g	3g	32mg	150mg	4g

RESTAURANT SELECTION

Tortilla Soup
from Yucatan, Mexico

The Tack Room
2800 Sabino Canyon Road
Tucson

The Tack Room is housed in a fifty-three-year-old adobe hacienda, nestled in the desert with a spectacular mountain view. Since its opening in 1965, it has established itself as one of the region's leading restaurants.

8 corn tortillas
oil for frying
1/2 C. onion, chopped
2 cloves garlic, crushed
1 (4-oz.) can chopped green chiles
1 (28-oz.) can solid pack tomatoes, pureed in blender
6 C. chicken broth
1-1/2 C. shredded cooked chicken
2 T. lime juice
salt, optional

Garnish
chopped cilantro leaves
grated mild cheddar or Monterey Jack cheese

Cut tortillas into 1/2-inch strips and fry in hot oil until crisp. Drain and set aside. In a large sauce pan, heat a small amount of oil and add onions, garlic and green chiles. Sauté until just golden. Do not let onions burn. Add tomatoes, chicken broth and shredded chicken and cover. Simmer slowly for about 15 minutes. Stir in lime juice and add salt if desired.

To serve: In the bottom of each serving bowl, place a handful of the prepared tortilla strips. Ladle the soup over the tortilla strips and top with cilantro and grated cheese.

Serves: 8

Cream of Green Chile Soup

Smooth and creamy, but mildly spicy, this soup is one of our favorites. If you prefer something that you can sink your teeth into, add a cooked diced potato or corn.

1/2 C. onion, diced
3 T. butter or margarine
2 T. flour
1 (8-oz.) can green chiles, pureed
1 C. chicken broth
1 C. 2% low-fat milk

In a medium saucepan, sauté onion in butter until transparent. Add flour and stir until mixture thickens. Add green chili and continue stirring. Add broth and milk, stir until heated.

Serves: 4
Preparation Time: 20 minutes

Icebox Gazpacho

An Arizona cookbook wouldn't be complete without Gazpacho and this is a sure-fire summer refresher. Low in fat and high in nutrients--how can you go wrong?

5 med. tomatoes (about 1-1/4 lbs.), peeled and diced
16 oz. tomato juice
1 stalk celery, chopped
1 med. green pepper, chopped
1 cucumber, peeled, seeded and chopped
1 T. Worcestershire sauce
2 T. red wine vinegar
2 T. chopped fresh parsley

In a large bowl, combine all ingredients. Refrigerate for several hours to allow flavors to blend (preferably overnight). Serve chilled.

Serves: 6
Preparation Time: 20 minutes

Cal	Pro	Carb	Fat	Chol	Sod	Fib
46	2g	1g	0g	0mg	198mg	2g

Cream of Gazpacho

A tangy way to cool down on a hot summer day with a new twist to a traditional recipe.

6 med. tomatoes, peeled, chopped and pureed
1 C. sour cream or plain low-fat yogurt
1/2 C. milk
2 T. lemon juice
2 T. tomato paste
1 T. olive oil
1 avocado, peeled, seeded and pureed
1 cucumber, peeled, seeded and diced
2 T. dried parsley
1/4 tsp. pepper
1/4 tsp. dill weed

In the bowl of a food processor, blend tomatoes, sour cream, milk, lemon juice, tomato paste and oil. Pour into a large bowl and add avocado, cucumber, parsley, pepper and dill. Mix well and refrigerate several hours to allow flavors to merge. Serve chilled.

Serves: 6 to 8
Preparation Time: 15 minutes

Plain Ole Chili

This is a basic starter chili recipe for anyone just getting their taste buds warmed to flavors of the Southwest. For heartier tastes, begin here and season according to your own inclinations or try the Tortilla Flat Killer Chili recipe (p. 43).

1 lg. onion, chopped
1 T. vegetable oil
1 lb. lean ground beef
1 (15-1/2-oz.) can pinto beans, drained and rinsed
1 (14-1/2 oz.) can tomatoes, chopped
1 T. chili powder
1/4 tsp. garlic powder
1 tsp. salt
1 tsp. sugar
1/4 tsp. black pepper
1 T. Worcestershire sauce

In a large skillet sauté onions in oil until transparent. Add ground beef and cook until brown. Drain excess fat from pan and then add remaining ingredients. Stir, cover and simmer for 1 hour.

Serves: 6
Preparation Time: 1-1/2 hours

Cal	Pro	Carb	Fat	Chol	Sod	Fib
285	23g	26g	9g	33mg	524mg	9g

Vegetarian Chili

If you've been wanting an appealing way to increase the fiber in your diet, here's a tasty way to make a transition to meatless dining that's both colorful and delicious.

1 (14-1/2-oz.) can tomatoes, chopped
1 (6-oz.) can tomato paste
1 (15-1/2-oz.) can kidney beans, drained and rinsed
1 (15-1/2-oz.) can pinto beans, drained and rinsed
1 (10-oz.) pkg. frozen lima beans
1 (10-oz.) pkg. frozen corn
1 med. onion, chopped
1 green pepper, chopped
1 stalk celery, chopped
2 cloves garlic, minced
3 drops hot sauce
1 T. chili powder
1 tsp. Mexican oregano leaves
2 bay leaves

In a large saucepan, combine all ingredients, cover and simmer for 1-1/2 hours. Discard bay leaves and serve. Freeze extra for later.

Serves: 8 to 10
Preparation Time: 2 hours

Cal	Pro	Carb	Fat	Chol	Sod	Fib
212	12g	41g	1g	0mg	78mg	13g

Killer Chili

Tortilla Flat
Tortilla Flat, AZ

A trip down the Apache Trail wouldn't quite be complete without a stop at Tortilla Flat for a bowl of chef Bob Brock's world famous Killer Chili. Tortilla Flat is located on Tortilla Creek 18 miles northeast of Apache Junction on Highway 88. The drive passes through some of the world's most beautiful scenery.

1 (6-lb.) can crushed tomatoes
1/2 (6-lb.) can water
2 hot yellow peppers
4 long green chiles
6-8 serrano chiles
3 lg. onions

Spice Pac
1 oz. garlic powder
1 oz. onion salt
1 oz. crushed red pepper
1 oz. cayenne
1 oz. cumin
1 oz. oregano
3 oz. chili powder

2-1/2 lbs. ground beef
1 (6-lb.) can Ranch style beans

Put tomatoes and water in chili pot and heat. Finely dice chiles and onions, then add to chili pot. Add Spice Pac. Brown ground beef, drain, then add to chili pot. Cook until all veggies are tender. Then add beans. Simmer.

Note: The chili is best if you let it sit one night in fridge -- make it one day and serve it the next. If you want it hotter, double the number of serranos, if you want it milder, use less.

Serves: more people than you probably know

Apricot Fruit Compote

Use as a soup or a dessert. This luscious fruit compote is a certain delight.

1 (16-oz.) can apricot halves, with juice
1/2 C. half and half
1 tsp. lemon juice
1 tsp. vanilla extract
1 T. apricot brandy (optional)
1/2 C. raspberries
1/2 C. strawberries, sliced
1 C. melon balls

In a blender or food processor, puree apricots and juice until smooth. Stir in half and half until blended. Add lemon juice, vanilla and brandy. Refrigerate several hours or overnight for best flavor. Mix fruit into compote before serving.

Serves: 6 to 8
Preparation Time: 15 minutes

SALADS

Fresh vegetables grow in Arizona year round, providing a great variety of wonderful salad ingredients from which to choose. During the long hot summers, Arizonans search for ways to prepare meals without heating up the kitchen. You'll find many innovative salad ideas in this section, including some new twists on old favorites.

Corkscrew Gazpacho uses many of the traditional Southwestern Gazpacho soup ingredients in a tasty pasta salad. For an out-of-the-ordinary treat, try the Black Jack Salad, which uses one of our favorites -- black beans. Many of our salads are so hearty they can be meals all by themselves, such as the Mesa Chicken and Bean Salad. Others make wonderful accompaniments to any of the entrées.

Six Shooter Taco Salad

Bits of Sunset

Black Jack Salad

Sunshine Salad

Crossroads Cabbage Salad

Three Bean Salad

Corkscrew Gazpacho

The Boulders Grilled Shrimp Salad

Freshly Marinated Arizona Vegetables

Mesa Chicken and Bean Salad

Baja Salad

Fiesta Salad

Bow and Arrow Salad

Corn Lemon Salad

Six Shooter Taco Salad

This guacamole-style dressing is not only a wonderful accompaniment to this salad, but it gets rave reviews as a chip dip.

Salad
3 C. shredded iceberg lettuce
1 (3-oz.) can black olives, sliced
1 (15-1/2-oz.) can kidney beans, drained and rinsed
1 tomato, chopped

Dressing
1 avocado, peeled, seeded and mashed
2 T. green chiles, diced
6 oz. low-fat yogurt
2 T. vinegar
1/8 tsp. chili powder
1/8 tsp. garlic powder

Topping
1/2 C. coarsely crushed corn chips
1/2 C. cheddar cheese, grated

In a large bowl, combine all salad ingredients. Toss. In a small bowl, blend together dressing ingredients. Pour dressing over salad. Sprinkle with topping.

Serves: 4
Preparation Time: 20 minutes

Bits of Sunset

Here's a pleasant vegetable combo that substitutes for a traditional lettuce salad. With only one tablespoon of oil, it's low in fat and calories.

Salad
1 red pepper, diced
2 carrots, sliced
1 lb. jicama, peeled and sliced
1 sm. onion, chopped

Dressing
1/3 C. red wine vinegar
1 T. olive oil
1 T. fresh cilantro, chopped
1 tsp. garlic powder
1/4 tsp. celery seed
1 T. sugar

In a medium bowl, place salad ingredients. In a small bowl, whisk together dressing ingredients. When blended, pour over vegetables and toss. Refrigerate until thoroughly chilled.

Serves: 6
Preparation Time: 15 minutes

Black Jack Salad

Arizonan's take the heat out of the kitchen by preparing foods that do not require cooking. Here's a tasty way to start a meal.

Salad
1 (8-oz.) can black beans
1 C. frozen peas, thawed
1 tomato, diced
1/4 C. red pepper, chopped
2 green onions (scallions), chopped
2 oz. green chiles, diced

Dressing
2 T. red wine vinegar
1 T. Dijon mustard
1/4 tsp. ground cumin
1/4 tsp. celery seed
1 T. olive oil
1 tsp. sugar

In a medium bowl, combine salad ingredients. In a small bowl, combine dressing ingredients and whisk together. Pour over vegetables and refrigerate until chilled. Before serving stir from the bottom to incorporate dressing.

Serves: 4
Preparation Time: 15 minutes

Cal	Pro	Carb	Fat	Chol	Sod	Fib
161	8g	24g	4g	0mg	98mg	3g

Sunshine Salad

A refreshing summer salad with a tangy taste that's loaded with Vitamin C.

Salad
6 oz. shell pasta, cooked and cooled
1 avocado, peeled and cubed
1/2 C. sliced almonds
1 orange, peeled and cut in 1/2-inch wedges
1/4 C. fresh parsley, chopped

Dressing
1/4 C. lime juice
1 T. honey

In a large bowl, combine salad ingredients. In a small bowl, whisk together dressing ingredients. Pour over pasta mixture, toss and chill.

Serves: 6
Preparation Time: 20 minutes

Crossroads Cabbage Salad

Country folks and city folks alike enjoy potlucks and picnics as a way to share good food and good times. This salad carries and stores well for those fun occasions.

Salad
1 lg. head cabbage, shredded
1 green pepper, diced
2 stalks celery, diced
1 C. red onion, diced

Dressing
1/3 C. sugar
2/3 C. vinegar
1/4 C. vegetable oil
1/2 tsp. salt
1/2 tsp. pepper

In a large bowl, combine salad ingredients. In a small saucepan, combine all dressing ingredients. Bring to a boil, remove from heat and let cool 5 minutes. Pour over cabbage mixture. Chill thoroughly before serving.

Serves: 8 to 10
Preparation Time: 30 minutes

Three Bean Salad

Looking for a fresh twist to a traditional favorite? Try our version with fresh green beans and garbanzos.

Salad
3/4 C. red onion, chopped
1 med. green pepper, chopped
1-1/4 C. garbanzo beans
1/2 lb. fresh green beans, cooked
1 (15-1/2-oz.) can kidney beans, drained and rinsed

Dressing
1 T. olive oil
1/2 C. red wine vinegar
3 T. sugar
dash pepper
dash garlic powder

In a large bowl, combine all salad ingredients. In a small bowl, whisk together dressing ingredients. Pour over beans and mix well. Chill thoroughly before serving.

Serves: 8
Preparation Time: 30 minutes

Cal	Pro	Carb	Fat	Chol	Sod	Fib
132	6g	22g	3g	0mg	6mg	6g

Corkscrew Gazpacho

With ingredients reminiscent of gazpacho, this salad provides a pasta version of that light and cool refreshment so welcome on a warm summer day.

Salad
8 oz. rotini, cooked and cooled
8 oz. button mushrooms
5 green onions (scallions), chopped
1 T. fresh parsley, chopped
1 cucumber, peeled, seeded and sliced
1/2 green pepper, cut in 1-inch strips
1/2 red pepper, cut in 1-inch strips
3 tomatoes, cut in wedges

Dressing
5 T. white vinegar
1/4 tsp. garlic powder
2 T. vegetable oil
1/2 tsp. basil
1 T. sugar
dash black pepper
1/3 C. mayonnaise
1 T. taco sauce
2 T. water

In a large bowl, combine rotini and all other salad ingredients. In a small bowl, whisk together dressing ingredients until well-blended. Pour dressing over salad, toss and chill thoroughly before serving.

Serves: 6
Preparation Time: 20 minutes

Grilled Shrimp Salad

The Boulders
Cantina del Pedregal
34361 N. Darlington Drive
Carefree

16 shrimp (1 oz. each), peeled and deveined
1 recipe Tomato Cumin Vinaigrette (recipe follows)
1 head iceberg lettuce
2 lg. ripe tomatoes, peeled and seeded, cut in 1/2-inch dice
8 croutons (thin slices baguette, lightly toasted)
Ancho Chili Aioli as needed (recipe follows)
1 lemon, cut in 8 wedges
1 each fresh sweet corn, cut off cob
1 C. cooked black beans
1 T. parsley, chopped

Marinate shrimp in the Tomato Cumin Vinaigrette 4 to 6 hours. Pre-heat barbecue grill (or use a Jennaire). Shred iceberg lettuce and toss with some of the Vinaigrette; divide between 4 plates mounding it up in the middle. Sprinkle diced tomato around the perimeter of the lettuce.

Spread croutons liberally with Ailoi and position on opposite sides of the plate; place one lemon wedge next to each crouton. Grill shrimp until barely done; slice lengthwise and toss with corn, black beans and a little of the vinaigrette. Mound equal amounts of the shrimp/corn/bean mixture on top of the lettuce and sprinkle with chopped parsley. Serve warm.

Ancho Chile Aioli
3 egg yolks
2 tsp. Dijon mustard
1/4 tsp. kosher salt
2 cloves garlic, minced
6 T. Ancho Chile Puree*
1/2 C. olive oil
1 T. balsamic vinegar
1 tsp. lemon juice

* Ancho Chile Puree--2 ancho chiles, stems removed, broken into pieces. Soak in 1/2 cup hot water. Puree in blender. If you'd like, add one red pepper, roasted, peeled and seeded.

Tomato Cumin Vinaigrette
1 tsp. fresh oregano, finely chopped
1 tsp fresh thyme, finely chopped
1 T. fresh basil, finely chopped
1/4 onion, minced
2 cloves garlic, minced
2 ripe tomatoes, peeled, seeded, roughly chopped
1/3 C. red wine vinegar
1 C. salad oil
1/2 C. tomato sauce
freshly toasted and ground cumin to taste

Blend all ingredients, season to taste and refrigerate.

Serves: 4

Chef Charles Wiley

Freshly Marinated Arizona Vegetables

Even the kids will find vegetables a tempting fare, when saturated with this zesty dressing.

Salad
1 head cauliflower, broken into flowerets
1 bunch broccoli, chopped in pieces
1 med. jicama, cubed
1 lg. red onion, sliced in rings
1/2 C. grated carrot

Dressing
1 tsp. lemon juice
1 T. dry mustard
1 T. Worcestershire sauce
1/2 tsp. white pepper
1 C. wine vinegar
1/4 tsp. garlic powder
1/4 C. sugar
1/2 C. water
1 tsp. salt
1/2 C. vegetable oil
3 drops hot sauce

Combine vegetables. Blend dressing ingredients well and pour over vegetables. Chill several hours and serve.

Serves: 8
Preparation Time: 20 minutes

Mesa Chicken and Bean Salad

On a hot summer day, you can keep the kitchen cool with this one-dish meal. With a tasty yogurt dressing this salad travels well to a picnic or a potluck!

Salad
1 med. red pepper, chopped
1 Anaheim chili, skinned, seeded and chopped
1 cucumber, peeled, seeded and chopped
6 radishes, sliced
2 green onions (scallions), chopped
3 boneless, skinless chicken breasts, cooked and diced
1 (15-1/2-oz.) can kidney beans, drained and rinsed

Dressing
1/4 C. red wine vinegar
1 T. sugar
1/2 tsp. garlic powder
1/4 tsp. celery seed
1 C. plain low-fat yogurt
1/2 tsp. dried parsley
1/4 tsp. coriander

In a large bowl, combine salad ingredients. In a medium bowl, combine all dressing ingredients and whisk until well-blended. Pour over salad. Toss and chill until ready to serve.

Serves: 8
Preparation Time: 30 minutes

Cal	Pro	Carb	Fat	Chol	Sod	Fib
144	14g	14g	3g	30mg	52mg	5g

Baja Salad

Pick the oranges right from an Arizona orange tree. This unusual combination of onions and oranges will please your palate.

Salad
4 oranges, peeled and sectioned
1 C. red onion, sliced in thin rings
4 oz. Monterey Jack cheese, cut in 1/2-inch cubes

Dressing
1 T. sugar
1 T. tarragon vinegar
1 tsp. celery seed
1/2 tsp. prepared mustard
1 tsp. salt
dash pepper
1 C. plain low-fat yogurt

6 C. salad greens (any variety)

In a large bowl, combine oranges, onion rings and cheese. In a small bowl, whisk together sugar, vinegar, celery seed, mustard, salt and pepper. Fold in yogurt. Set aside. Pour dressing over orange/cheese mixture and combine well. Chill for 1 hour before serving.

Tear greens into bite size pieces and place in a salad bowl. Serve with orange-cheese mixture on top.

Serves: 6
Preparation Time. 1 hour and 15 minutes

Cal	Pro	Carb	Fat	Chol	Sod	Fib
169	9g	20g	7g	20mg	492mg	3g

Fiesta Salad

This salad features jicama, a delightful Mexican vegetable which adds a crunchy sweet taste. Difficult to describe, but a must-try.

Salad
1 med. red onion, sliced into rings
1 cucumber, seeded and diced
1 med. jicama, peeled and julienned

Dressing
2 T. lemon juice
1 1/2 T. lime juice
1/4 tsp. lemon peel
3 T. oil-free Italian dressing
2 tsp. sugar

2 C. shredded iceberg lettuce

In a large bowl, combine onion, cucumber and jicama. In a small bowl, whisk together all dressing ingredients. Pour dressing over cucumber-jicama mixture and stir until all the vegetables are coated. Arrange on a bed of shredded lettuce and serve.

Serves: 6
Preparation Time: 15 minutes

Cal	Pro	Carb	Fat	Chol	Sod	Fib
42	1g	9g	1g	0mg	44mg	1g

Bow and Arrow Salad

This refreshingly cool pasta salad can be prepared ahead. It will keep for several days in the refrigerator.

Salad
8 oz. bow tie pasta, cooked and cooled
1 med. tomato, diced
1/2 C. red onion, chopped
1/2 green pepper, cut in 1-inch pieces
1/2 red pepper, cut in 1-inch pieces
1/2 C. black olives, sliced

Dressing
1/2 C. mayonnaise
1/2 C. plain yogurt
1/2 tsp. chili powder

In a large bowl, combine salad ingredients. Whisk together dressing ingredients until well-blended. Pour over vegetable-pasta mixture and toss. Serve chilled.

Serves: 5 to 6
Preparation Time: 20 minutes

Corn Lemon Salad

A delightful intermingling of spices flavor this versatile side dish. Serve as a salad or as a relish.

Salad
1-1/2 C. tomatoes, peeled, seeded and chopped
1 C. cucumber, peeled, seeded and chopped
3/4 C. sweet corn (fresh or frozen)
1/3 C. yellow pepper, chopped
1/3 C. red pepper, chopped
2/3 C. red onion, chopped
3 T. green onions (scallions), chopped

Dressing
1 T. sugar
1/4 tsp. celery seed
1/8 tsp. each cinnamon, nutmeg and black pepper
dash ground cloves
1/2 C. lemon juice

In a large bowl, combine salad ingredients. Sprinkle with sugar, celery seed, cinnamon, nutmeg, pepper and cloves. Drizzle with lemon juice. Mix well. Serve chilled.

Serves: 6
Preparation Time: 20 minutes

Cal	Pro	Carb	Fat	Chol	Sod	Fib
55	2g	12g	0g	0g	6mg	2g

VEGETABLES, RICE AND BEANS

Rice and beans have become staples in the Arizona diet, reflecting the Spanish and Native American influences on the state's culinary arts. Among the recipes in this section you'll find many that answer the needs of special diets. When creatively prepared, bean dishes can be delicious sources of protein, minerals, and cholesterol-reducing fiber.

Mexican Maze is a great way to put some pizazz into corn. Diablo Rice and Chicken could easily be a meal all by itself. The Dreamy Draw Rice and Honey doubles as a dessert. And you're sure to change the minds of the non-bean eaters once they try our Campfire Beans.

Mexican Maze

Roustabout Corn Kernels

Outpost Potato Medley

Creamy Emerald Peppers

Spinach and Rice Casserole

Diablo Rice and Chicken

Peppered Rice Dressing

Dreamy Draw Rice and Honey

Saffron Rice

Pinon Rice

Juarez Rice

Rawhide Cowboy Beans

Midnight Beans

Campfire Beans

Rattler's Beans

Black Bean Tostada

Drunken Beans

Hangman's Refried Black Beans

Mexican Maze

You'll be amazed at how good this Mexican-style corn dish tastes.

1 sm. onion, chopped
1 clove garlic, minced
2 T. butter or margarine
1 (4-oz.) can green chiles, diced
2 C. frozen corn
1/2 C. milk
1/2 C. cheddar cheese, grated

In a large skillet over medium heat, sauté onion and garlic in butter until the onion is transparent. Add the chiles and corn and sauté until heated through. Turn heat to low. Add cheese and milk and continue stirring. Serve when cheese is melted.

Serves: 4
Preparation Time: 20 minutes

Roustabout Corn Kernels

Whether you use fresh, frozen or canned corn, this side dish will add zest to any meal.

1 sm. onion, chopped
1 clove garlic, minced
1/2 T. vegetable oil
2 C. corn
2 T. lime juice
1/3 C. prepared salsa (or Thick and Chunky Salsa, p. 20)

In a medium skillet, sauté onion and garlic in oil until transparent. Add corn. Simmer until heated through. Add lime juice and salsa.

Serves: 4
Preparation Time: 10 minutes

Cal	Pro	Carb	Fat	Chol	Sod	Fib
97	3g	18g	2g	0mg	99mg	3g

Outpost Potato Medley

Use as a side dish or add a slice of bread and fresh fruit and you'll have a complete meatless meal.

1 med. onion, sliced
2 cloves garlic, minced
1/2 T. vegetable oil
1 tsp. dried coriander
2 potatoes, cubed
1 (15-1/2-oz.) can pinto beans
1 T. freshly squeezed lemon juice
1-1/2 C. water
6 oz. fresh spinach, cleaned and trimmed

In a large skillet, sauté onion and garlic in oil until onion is transparent. Add coriander. Stir. Add potatoes, beans, lemon juice, water and spinach. Bring to a boil, then simmer for 40 minutes.

Serves: 4 to 6
Preparation Time: 55 minutes

Cal	Pro	Carb	Fat	Chol	Sod	Fib
247	10g	36g	2g	0mg	25mg	10g

Creamy Emerald Peppers

The crunchiness of the green peppers are a scrumptious contrast to the smoothness of the creamed rice.

6 green peppers
8 oz. sour cream, or plain low-fat yogurt
2 tsp. prepared mustard
1/4 C. onion, chopped
2 C. cooked white rice
1 C. cheddar cheese, grated

Preheat oven to 350°F. Cut tops off peppers, remove seeds. In a large saucepan, bring water to a boil and add peppers. Parboil for 3 minutes until the peppers turn bright green. Drain.

In a small mixing bowl, combine sour cream, mustard and onion. Add rice. Mix well.Place peppers in a shallow baking dish. Fill with rice mixture. Top with cheese and bake for 30 minutes.

Serves: 6
Preparation Time: 45 minutes

Spinach and Rice Casserole

This dish has all the makings of a one-dish meal--protein and complex carbohydrates, and it's also low in fat.

2 C. cooked white rice
8 oz. cottage cheese
1 (10-oz.) pkg. frozen chopped spinach, thawed and drained
2 eggs
1/2 tsp. salt
dash of pepper

Preheat oven to 350°F. Spray a large baking dish with non-stick vegetable spray. Combine all ingredients and spoon into baking dish. Bake 30 minutes.

Serves: 4 to 6 (main dish), 8 (side dish)
Preparation Time: 45 minutes

Cal	Pro	Carb	Fat	Chol	Sod	Fib
116	8g	17g	2g	75mg	316mg	1g

Diablo Rice and Chicken

This tomato-flavored one skillet rice dish is a complete casserole meal. Colorful, delicious and nutritious.

2 C. fresh mushrooms, cleaned and sliced
1 med. onion, chopped
3/4 C. green pepper, chopped
1 stalk celery, chopped
1 C. grated carrot
1 T. olive oil
1/2 C. cucumber, peeled, seeded and diced
1 (15-oz.) can tomato puree
3-3/4 C. chicken broth
1-1/4 C. white rice, uncooked
3 boneless, skinless chicken breasts, cooked and diced

In a large skillet, sauté mushrooms, onion, green pepper, celery and carrot in olive oil. Add cucumber, tomato puree and 3/4 cup of broth to the vegetable mixture. Bring to a boil. Add remaining broth and rice. Return to a boil, then turn down heat and simmer for 15 minutes. Add chicken and cook for 5 minutes.

Serves: 8
Preparation Time: 35 minutes

Cal	Pro	Carb	Fat	Chol	Sod	Fib
188	12g	25g	5g	28mg	684mg	3g

Peppered Rice Dressing

The perfect side dish or stuffing for your Thanksgiving Day turkey, this easy-to-prepare rice dish will be popular.

2 cloves garlic, minced
1/2 red pepper, chopped
1/2 green pepper, chopped
1 Anaheim chile, skinned, seeded and chopped
3 ears fresh corn, kernels cut from cob
1/2 T. vegetable oil
2 C. white rice, cooked
1 T. fresh cilantro, chopped
1/2 tsp. chili powder

In a large skillet, sauté garlic, peppers, chile and corn in oil. Add rice, cilantro and chili powder. Heat thoroughly.

Serves: 6
Preparation Time: 30 minutes

Cal	Pro	Carb	Fat	Chol	Sod	Fib
175	4g	34g	2g	0mg	6mg	2g

Dreamy Draw Rice and Honey

This tasty rice dish is tempting enough to be a dessert alternative to cake and cookies.

2 C. brown rice, cooked and cooled
1/2 C. dates, chopped
2 T. honey
1/2 C. pecans, chopped
1 C. pineapple chunks, drained
1/4 tsp. nutmeg
1/4 tsp. cinnamon

In a large bowl, combine all ingredients. Chill and serve.

Serves: 6
Preparation Time: 15 minutes

Cal	Pro	Carb	Fat	Chol	Sod	Fib
245	3g	46g	7g	0mg	187mg	3g

Saffron Rice

Saffron, the world's most expensive spice (it takes the stigmas of 70,000 crocus flowers to yield one pound of saffron) makes this dish as pretty as a picture while adding a delicate flavor.

3 C. cooked white rice
1/2 tsp. saffron
3 cloves garlic, minced
1 med. onion, chopped
2 T. butter
1/2 green pepper, diced
1/2 red pepper, diced
1/4 C. tomato, peeled, seeded and chopped

In a large bowl, combine rice and saffron. Mix well. In a large skillet, sauté garlic and onion in butter until transparent. Add rice and vegetables to skillet. Cover and heat through. Serve warm.

Serves: 6
Preparation Time: 20 minutes

Pinon Rice

You'll enjoy the distinctive flavor the pine nuts lend to this recipe.

1 T. butter or margarine
1 med. onion, chopped
2 cloves garlic, minced
1 Anaheim chile, peeled, seeded and cut into 1-inch strips
1 red bell pepper, cut into 1-inch strips
1/4 C. pine nuts (pinons)
1-1/2 C. cooked white rice
1 C. frozen corn
1 C. sour cream (or plain low-fat yogurt)
1/4 tsp. ground cumin

In a large skillet, melt butter over medium heat. Add onion, garlic, chile, pepper and pine nuts. Stir until nuts begin to brown. Add the remaining ingredients. Heat through.

Serves: 6
Preparation Time: 15 minutes

Juarez Rice

This colorful rice dish will complement any entrée.

1/2 T. vegetable oil
1 lg. onion, chopped
2 T. garlic, minced
2 C. cooked white rice
1 C. chicken or vegetable broth
3 med. tomatoes, peeled, seeded and chopped
1/8 tsp. dried coriander
1 C. frozen peas

In a large skillet, sauté onions and garlic in oil until transparent. Add rice and sauté until coated with oil. Add broth and tomatoes. Cover and simmer 5 minutes until liquid is completely absorbed. Add coriander and peas. Simmer 5 additional minutes.

Serves: 4 to 6
Preparation Time: 20 minutes

Cal	Pro	Carb	Fat	Chol	Sod	Fib
152	5g	30g	2g	0mg	198mg	3g

Rawhide Cowboy Beans

Rawhide Steakhouse and Saloon
23023 N. Scottsdale Road
Scottsdale

Rawhide is Arizona's largest 1880s western theme attraction providing entertainment for the entire family including stagecoach rides, gold panning and a shooting gallery. The restaurant is known for its mesquite-broiled steak and barbecue chicken and features popular country music and dancing.

1 lb. dry pinto beans
water to cover beans
3 qts. water
1/4 lb. salt pork or diced bacon (ham may be substituted)
1 T. sugar
1/2 tsp. paprika
1 tsp. white pepper
1/2 tsp. hot sauce

Cover beans with water and soak overnight. Drain. Sauté bacon over low heat for 5 minutes. Add 3 quarts water, bacon, drained beans and remainder of ingredients. Bring to a boil, cover and simmer for 2-1/2 to 3 hours, until beans are tender.

Serves: 8 to 10

Midnight Beans

These savory black beans are a superb complement to a chicken or fish entrée.

1 C. canned black beans, rinsed and drained
2 Roma tomatoes, chopped
1/4 C. fresh cilantro, chopped
1/4 C. fresh parsley, chopped
1/2 C. balsamic vinegar

In a large skillet, combine beans, tomatoes, cilantro, parsley and vinegar. Simmer 20 minutes.

Serves: 6
Preparation Time: 20 minutes

Cal	Pro	Carb	Fat	Chol	Sod	Fib
67	4g	14g	0g	0mg	250mg	1g

Campfire Beans

You don't have to be a bean lover to enjoy this dish. This recipe can easily be doubled for company.

1 (15-1/2-oz.) can pinto beans, drained and rinsed
1 lg. onion, chopped
2 tsp. garlic, minced
1-1/2 C. canned tomatoes, chopped
1 (4-oz.) can green chiles, diced
1/4 C. taco sauce
1/2 tsp. cumin
dash of pepper

Combine all ingredients. Cook covered over medium heat for 20 minutes. Remove cover and cook 5 minutes more to reduce liquid.

Serves: 4
Preparation Time: 30 minutes

Cal	Pro	Carb	Fat	Chol	Sod	Fib
217	12g	43g	1g	0mg	348mg	13g

RESTAURANT SELECTION

Rattler's Beans

Rattler's Restaurant at WestWorld
16601 N. Pima Road
Scottsdale

Ain't nothing like it. With plates so big, they dare ya' to finish, Rattler's steakhouse and saloon offers entertainment, dancing and live country music to accompany your meal.

1-1/2 lbs. dried pinto beans
4 oz. chopped bacon
6 oz. green chiles, diced
3/4 lb. Spanish onions, diced
1/2 lb. celery, diced small
2 oz. ham base
1/2 oz. beef base
1 T. granulated garlic
3 tsp. salt
1 T. black pepper
3 tsp. chile powder
1 tsp. crushed red pepper

Soak beans in water overnight. Simmer beans in water until done. While the beans are simmering, cook bacon until done, then add the vegetables to the bacon grease with the bacon still in the pan. Cook vegetables until done.

Add the cooked bacon, bases, seasonings, vegetables and bacon drippings to the beans. Let it simmer for 1 hour. Yields 1-1/2 gallons of beans.

Serves: 21

Black Bean Tostada

Who says what's good for you has to taste bad? These tostadas are high in vitamins and minerals and are absolutely delicious. We've made them again and again for family and friends.

1 med. onion, chopped
2 cloves garlic, minced
1/2 T. vegetable oil
1(8-oz.) can black beans, including juice
1 C. canned tomatoes, chopped
1 C. frozen peas
dash of pepper
1/4 tsp. cumin
6 tortillas
3 oz. cheddar cheese, grated

In a large skillet, sauté onion and garlic in oil until transparent. Add beans and mash with a fork. Add tomatoes. Combine well. Add peas, pepper and cumin. Cook on medium heat 5 to 7 minutes, until liquid is absorbed.

Place tortillas in a plastic bag and warm in microwave 20 seconds on high. Place tortilla on plate and spread 1/4 cup of bean filling on each. Sprinkle with cheese and enjoy.

Serves: 6
Preparation Time: 20 minutes

Cal	Pro	Carb	Fat	Chol	Sod	Fib
313	15g	45g	7g	13mg	417mg	4g

Drunken Beans

This recipe calls for a half of a bottle of beer; the other half is for the cook. Seriously, though, the beer adds a distinctive flavor to the frijoles.

1 med. onion, chopped
2 cloves garlic, minced
1/2 T. vegetable oil
2 Anaheim chiles, peeled and chopped
1 (15-1/2-oz.) can pinto beans, drained and rinsed
1 (8-oz.) can tomato sauce
6 oz. Mexican beer
1 bouillon cube, vegetable or chicken
1 tsp. Mexican oregano leaves
1/4 tsp. ground cumin

Combine all ingredients. Bring to a boil and simmer for 30 minutes.

Serves: 6 to 8
Preparation Time: 40 minutes

Cal	Pro	Carb	Fat	Chol	Sod	Fiber
136	6g	24g	2g	0mg	311mg	7g

Hangman's Refried Black Beans

A great side dish with any meal. We recommend it with the Grilled Salmon with Pesto Sauce.

2 garlic cloves
1 med. onion, cut in pieces
1 green pepper, cut in pieces
1/2 T. olive oil
1 (15-1/2-oz.) can black beans
2 T. white wine
1 bay leaf
1 T. sugar
1 T. white vinegar
1 tsp. Mexican oregano leaves

In the bowl of a food processor, puree garlic, onion and pepper. In a medium skillet, sauté onion mixture in oil.
In a small bowl, mash beans with a fork. Add to onion mixture. Add remaining ingredients. Cook over medium heat until heated through. Discard bay leaf.

Serves: 4 to 6
Preparation Time: 20 minutes

Cal	Pro	Carb	Fat	Chol	Sod	Fib
164	9g	29g	2mg	0mg	250mg	2g

CHEESE AND EGG ENTREES

Even though the American public has become somewhat reluctant to indulge in cheese and eggs, any of these recipes can be made by using an egg substitute or the low-fat or non-fat milk version of regular cheese. Eggs and cheese both provide protein, and cheese is a good source of calcium.

From sunrise to sunset you'll find a tempting Arizona favorite to see you on your way. Start with the Huevos Rancheros Frittata for breakfast. If it's Sunday brunch that's on your agenda, try the Kinfolk Bean Casserole. Cheese Crisps are perfect for snacking. Throw a party and serve the delicious deep dish Mexican Pizza. With these tasty dishes, you've got every meal covered!

Cheese Crisp

Cheese Enchiladas

Friday Night Quiche

Huevos Rancheros Fritatta

Los Dos Molinos Blue Corn Stacked Enchiladas

Mexican Pizza

Kinfolk Bean Casserole

Sunrise Eggs with Vegetables

Cheese Crisp

Arizonans have cheese crisps as an appetizer, a snack or a meal. It's a fast and satisfying when you have no time to cook.

1 lg. flour tortilla
1/2 C. cheddar cheese, grated
1/2 C. Monterey Jack cheese, grated
1 Anaheim chile, peeled, seeded and diced
1/2 C. black olives, sliced
1/2 red pepper, chopped
1 C. prepared salsa

Preheat broiler. Spray a large baking sheet with non-stick vegetable spray. On the baking sheet, place tortilla. Layer cheeses, then arrange remaining ingredients on top. Place under the broiler for 5 minutes or until cheese is melted. Slice in wedges. Serve with salsa.

Serves: 4
Preparation Time: 10 minutes

Cheese Enchiladas

This is a quick and easy way to make enchiladas. You'll keep the house cool and have only one dish to clean up.

1-1/2 C. Monterey Jack cheese, grated
4 green onions, chopped
1 (4-oz.) can green chiles, diced
3 eggs, slightly beaten
8 (10-inch) flour tortillas
1 (19-oz.) can enchilada sauce
1/2 C. cheddar cheese, grated

Spray a 9" x 13" baking dish with non-stick vegetable spray. In a medium bowl, combine Monterey Jack, onions, chiles and eggs. Lay a tortilla on a flat surface and spoon in 2 tablespoons of the cheese mixture in a narrow strip down the center. Roll up, leaving ends open. Place in baking dish. Repeat for remaining tortillas.

Pour 1 cup of the enchilada sauce over the tortillas. Microwave on high for 10 minutes, uncovered. Pour all but 1/2 cup of the sauce over and return to the microwave for another 10 minutes. Pour on the rest of the sauce, sprinkle with cheddar cheese and microwave on high for 1-1/2 minutes.

Serves: 4 to 6
Preparation Time: 30 minutes

Friday Night Quiche

*A quiche is a quiche, but this is a **quiche**! The unique combination of chiles and oysters will make this a delicacy that you won't soon forget. Fat and cholesterol reducing substitutes are given in parenthesis.*

1 (8-inch) uncooked pie crust
8 oz. cream cheese (or light cream cheese)
1 C. milk (or skim milk)
4 eggs (or 1 C. egg substitute)
1 (8-oz.) can oysters, drained
4 oz. green chiles, diced

Preheat oven to 350°F. Place pie crust in an 8" pie pan and crimp the edges. Soften cream cheese by heating in the microwave for 35 seconds. In a medium-sized bowl, add milk and eggs to the cream cheese. Using an electric mixer, blend until the cream cheese is completely incorporated.

Drain oysters and chiles and arrange in a single layer in the bottom of the pie crust. Pour the egg-cheese mixture into the pie crust. Bake 60 minutes. Use a cake tester to test for doneness.

Serves: 8
Preparation Time: 1 hour and 10 minutes

Huevos Rancheros Fritatta

Prepare the sauce ahead of time and you're ready for an enticing Sunday brunch in just a few minutes.

Sauce
1 T. vegetable oil
1 sm. onion, chopped
1 clove garlic, minced
1 Anaheim chile, peeled, seeded and chopped
1 (15-oz.) can tomatoes, drained and chopped (reserve 1/4 C. liquid)
1/4 C. taco sauce

Egg Mixture
4 eggs
1/4 C. milk
1 T. butter
1/2 C. cheddar cheese, grated

In a large skillet, heat oil and sauté the onion, garlic and chile. Add tomatoes, reserved liquid and taco sauce. Heat through. In a medium bowl, beat eggs and milk.

In a large skillet, melt butter over medium heat. Pour in egg mixture. Cook eggs for 3 minutes. Sprinkle with cheese. Cook 3 additional minutes. Spread sauce over eggs and heat through.

Serves: 2
Preparation Time: 15 minutes

RESTAURANT SELECTION

Blue Corn Stacked Enchiladas

Los Dos Molinos
260 W. Alma School Road
1156 W. Main Street
Mesa

The Chavez family has brought classic flavors of New Mexico to Arizona. If you like it hot, you'll want to try this dish.

Blue Corn Tortillas
4 C. blue corn masa
2 tsp. garlic salt
1/2 tsp. pepper
1 C. water

Combine ingredients to a pie crust texture. Divide into 15 to 20 1-1/2-inch balls. Use tortilla press to make corn tortillas and fry on a hot griddle with just enough oil to keep from sticking.

Red Chili Sauce
15 to 20 New Mexico chili pods
4 cloves garlic
1/2 tsp. cumin
1 tsp. oregano
5 C. beef or chicken broth
corn starch
salt and pepper to taste

Soak chiles overnight in water. Add garlic to chiles and blend until pureed. Bring broth to a boil and add remaining sauce ingredients. Add pureed chili sauce, bring to a boil. Thicken with corn starch.

Blue Corn Enchiladas

Blue Corn Tortillas
Red Chili Sauce
cheese
onion
meat (beef, pork, chicken)
egg (fried)

Make enchiladas individually by taking your cooked corn tortillas cover with Red Chili Sauce add cheeses and onion and continue to stack to your desired height (usually 3) alternating chili, cheese and onion. You can use any type of roast, chicken or pork if you like. Traditionally, this dinner comes topped with an egg as so many New Mexican entrées are. Serve with a side of beans and you have a very authentic New Mexican dinner.

Serves: 15 to 20

Mexican Pizza

If you like pizza, you'll enjoy this deep-dish Mexican version with Monterey Jack cheese. The pizza crust is easy to prepare and has a distinctive homemade taste.

1 T. yeast
1 tsp. sugar
1 C. warm water
2 to 3 cups flour
1 C. tomato sauce
3 oz. Monterey Jack cheese, grated
3 oz. cheddar cheese, grated
4 oz. can green chiles, diced
1/2 C. black olives, chopped

In a large bowl, combine yeast, sugar, water. Wait 4 to 7 minutes until the mixture bubbles to assure yeast is alive. Add 2 cups of flour and knead for 3 to 5 minutes. Add more flour if dough is sticky. Place dough in a bowl that has been sprayed with non-stick vegetable spray and cover with wax paper. Let rise for 1 hour.

Return dough to floured board and knead well for about 3 minutes. Roll dough out into a 9" X 13" rectangle and place in a baking dish. Let rise 45 to 60 minutes. Preheat oven to 450°F. Top pizza dough with tomato sauce, cheeses and toppings. Bake for 30 minutes.

Serves: 6
Preparation Time: 2-1/2 hours

Kinfolk Bean Casserole

This low-calorie quiche-style dish is a great way to introduce your kinfolk to an imaginative Southwestern Sunday brunch.

1 lg. onion, chopped
3 eggs (or egg substitute), beaten
1-1/2 C. canned evaporated skim milk
4 oz. cheddar cheese, grated
1 (4-oz.) can green chiles, diced
2 C. brown rice, cooked
1 (15-1/2-oz.) can kidney beans, drained and rinsed
1 C. low-fat cottage cheese

Preheat oven to 325°F. Spray a large casserole dish with non-stick vegetable spray. In a large bowl, combine all ingredients. Pour into prepared casserole dish. Bake for 45 minutes, or until a knife inserted in the center comes out clean. Let stand 10 minutes before serving.

Serves: 12
Preparation Time: 1 hour and 10 minutes

Sunrise Eggs with Vegetables

Here's an inviting alternative to bacon and eggs. Don't just serve this for breakfast, it also makes a hearty supper dish.

1 med. onion, chopped
1 clove garlic, minced
1 T. butter or margarine
2 med. potatoes, diced and cooked
2 med. tomatoes, peeled and chopped
1 red pepper, chopped
2 eggs
salt and pepper to taste

In a large skillet, sauté the onion and garlic in butter until transparent. Add potatoes, tomatoes and red pepper. Cook over medium heat until heated through. With a spoon, hollow out two large circles. Place one egg in each circle and continue cooking until eggs are set.

Serves: 2
Preparation Time: 30 minutes

FISH ENTREES

Despite Arizona's lack of shoreline, the state doesn't lack innovative ways of fixing the fruits of other shores. When combined with traditional Arizona seasonings, it doesn't take long to identify these dishes as specific to the region.

Whether you're looking for a new way to try a few of your favorite seafoods or an extra special way to turn a meal into a culinary experience, you'll find recipes made to order in this section. For a special occasion, try the Green Paillarde of Halibut in Mint and Southwestern Seasonings, which Chef Lenard R. Rubin serves at the Windows on the Green Restaurant at the world-class Phoenician resort. For a quick and easy meal, use your leftover cornbread to prepare one of our favorites -- Golden Scallops with Cornbread.

Back East Fish Supreme

Champagne Scallops

Westcourt in the Buttes Tarragon Seared Ono with Pineapple
Passion Fruit Glaze

Crab Enchiladas

Golden Scallops with Cornbread

Grilled Salmon with Pesto Sauce

The Phoenician Windows on the Green Paillarde of Halibut in
Mint and Southwestern Seasonings

Lemon Grilled Shrimp

Pescado Rojo

Scallops with Catalina Rice

The Phoenician Windows on the Green Grilled Mexican
Shrimp with Prickly Pear Cactus Fruit Vinaigrette

Shrimp Verde

Stone Springs Salmon Tarts

White Fish in Almond and Cilantro

Zesty Snapper

Back East Fish Supreme

Tender, moist and flavorful. Fish prepared in this manner is sure to be a crowd pleaser.

2 lg. onions, finely chopped
3 stalks celery, cut into thin slices
3 T. fresh parsley, chopped (1 T. dried)
1 T. vegetable oil
1 tsp. Mexican oregano leaves
1/4 tsp. dry mustard
1/4 tsp. ground black pepper
2 lb. fillets of cod, flounder or any whitefish
1/2 C. sharp cheddar cheese, grated
1 (16-oz.) can tomato sauce
1/2 C. crushed corn flakes or dry bread crumbs

Preheat oven to 350°F. Spray a large baking dish with non-stick vegetable spray. In a large skillet, sauté onion, celery, and parsley in oil until tender. Add oregano, mustard and pepper.

Spread half of the onion mixture on the bottom of the baking dish. Layer fish over this and spread remaining onion mixture on top. Sprinkle with cheese. Pour tomato sauce and spread with a spatula to completely cover cheese. Sprinkle with crumbs. Cover with foil and bake for 45 minutes. Sauce will be bubbling when done.

Serves: 6 to 8
Preparation Time: 1 hour

Cal	Pro	Carb	Fat	Chol	Sod	Fib
168	19g	6g	7g	39mg	527mg	1g

Champagne Scallops

This fricassee of scallops, with leek, red bell peppers and champagne sauce adds a festive holiday touch to any meal. While you're opening the New Year's Eve champagne, set aside a half cup for this recipe.

3 green onions,(scallions) minced
1 large leek, trimmed, halved and thinly sliced
1/3 C. red pepper, sliced
6 T. unsalted butter
2 lbs. large scallops
1/2 C. flour
1/2 C. champagne or sparkling white wine
1-1/2 C. whipping cream
1 T. lemon juice, freshly squeezed
1/8 tsp. hot sauce
1/3 C. Parmesan cheese, freshly grated
salt and pepper to taste
8 puff pastry shells or 8 oz. cooked linguini

In a large skillet, sauté green onions, leek and pepper in 2 tablespoons butter over medium-high heat until tender (about 4 minutes). Remove vegetables and set aside. Dredge scallops in flour. In the same skillet melt remaining butter and cook scallops until golden brown and just firm to the touch (about 5 minutes). Remove and set aside.

Pour champagne into the skillet. Boil until reduced by half, scraping in any brown bits. Add cream, lemon juice and hot sauce. Reduce heat and simmer until liquid is reduced to 1 cup (about 10 minutes). Stir in Parmesan cheese and reserved vegetables. Simmer until cheese mixture melts and the mixture is reduced to 1-1/2 cups (about 3 minutes). Return scallops to the sauce and reheat gently. Season with salt and pepper.

Serve over puff pastry shells or thin with half and half or milk and serve over linguini.

Serves: 8
Preparation Time: 30 minutes

RESTAURANT SELECTION

Tarragon Seared Ono
with Pineapple-Passion Fruit Glaze

Westcourt in the Buttes
Top of the Rock
2000 Westcourt Way
Tempe

Also known as king mackerel, ono is one of Hawaii's most flavorful fish. Firm, white, meaty and moist, ono in Hawaiian means, "The best, number one!"

Ono
2-1/4 lbs. ono, cut into 12 (1/2-inch thick) slices
1 qt. orange juice
1 C. flour
1 tsp. salt
2 T. dried tarragon leaves
1/2 tsp. garlic powder
pinch of white pepper
clarified butter, to coat pan

Pineapple-Passion Fruit Glaze
2 T. shallots, chopped
1 T. pickled ginger, chopped
1/2 C. pineapple, finely diced
1 qt. orange juice
1 C. passion fruit puree or juice
1/2 C. white wine
1/4 C. cream
1 lb. unsalted butter, in pieces, cold
salt and pepper to taste

Garnish
tropical fruit such as banana, kiwi, pineapple and papaya

Marinate 20 minutes and coat: Marinate the ono in orange juice. When done remove the fish from the marinade and blot dry. Coat with a mixture of flour, salt, tarragon, garlic powder and pepper.

Sauté: To avoid crowding, cook the fish in 2 pans or batches. Sauté in butter until light brown on both sides. When done, place the fish on a plate, and cover to keep warm. Keep the juices in the pan.

Sauté and simmer 25 to 35 minutes: In a clean saucepan, heat the original orange juice used to marinate the fish over medium heat until reduced by two thirds. In the fish pan, over a hot flame, sauté the shallots, ginger and pineapple. Cook until the shallots are translucent.

Add 1 qt. orange juice, passion fruit puree and white wine to the fish pan and reduce until thick. Add the cream and simmer until reduced by half. Keep the sauce at a simmer while adding the butter. Add the butter piece by piece, whisking constantly until incorporated. Salt and pepper to taste.

Reheat the fish: Return the fish to the glaze pan to rewarm and coat with glaze.

Serve: Serve on warm plates covered with Pineapple-Passion Fruit Glaze. Garnish with tropical fruit.

Serves: 6

Chef Franklin Biggs

Crab Enchiladas

Enchiladas are often filled with surprises. You'll be pleased to find the delicious taste of crab in these.

1-1/2 C. shredded crabmeat
1/2 C. Monterey Jack cheese, shredded
1 C. prepared salsa
2/3 C. celery, finely chopped
3 oz. cream cheese
1/2 C. green onions (scallions), sliced
1/2 tsp. garlic salt
8 (6-inch) flour tortillas

Garnish
1/2 C. Monterey Jack cheese
1 C. shredded iceberg lettuce
1/2 C. black olives, sliced
1 C. prepared salsa

Preheat oven to 350°F. Spray a large baking dish with non-stick vegetable oil. In a large bowl, combine crabmeat, 1/2 cup Monterey Jack, 1/3 cup salsa, celery, cream cheese, onions and salt.

In the center of each tortilla, spoon 1/3 cup of the crab mixture. Roll up and place in baking dish. Spoon remaining salsa over enchiladas. Cover with foil and bake for 20 minutes. Sprinkle remaining cheese on top to garnish. Serve topped with lettuce, sliced olives and more salsa.

Serves: 4
Preparation Time: 40 minutes

Golden Scallops with Cornbread

Palate-pleasing, this is a tasty example of sophisticated Southwest cooking.

4 T. butter or margarine
1 med. onion, chopped
3 cloves garlic, minced
2 oz. green chiles, diced
salt and pepper to taste

1 C. cornbread, crumbled (see p. 150 for Ultissimo Mexican
        Cornbread)
1 lb. scallops
2 T. parsley, chopped

In a large skillet, melt 2 tablespoons of the butter. Sauté the
onion and garlic until onion is transparent. Add chiles, salt
and pepper. Sauté a few more minutes. Remove from skillet
and set aside. Melt the remaining butter and sauté cornbread
crumbs until golden brown. Set aside with the onion mixture.

Sauté scallops, stirring constantly until they turn white. Add
cornbread/onion mixture. Heat until all moisture is absorbed.
Sprinkle with parsley and serve.

Serves: 4
Preparation Time: 15 to 20 minutes

Grilled Salmon with Pesto Sauce

*When you see the irresistible bright pink salmon at the fish
market, you'll want to prepare it in a special way. We
recommend serving Hangman's Refried Black Beans with
this dish (see p. 74 for recipe).*

Pesto Sauce
3 T. dried basil
1/4 C. dried parsley (begin with fresh and dry overnight)
2 T. vegetable oil
2 T. vinegar
1/4 C. freshly ground Parmesan cheese
3 cloves garlic, chopped
dash pepper

1 lb. salmon fillet

In the bowl of a food processor, puree all ingredients except
the salmon. Pour pesto sauce over salmon and marinate in
refrigerator at least one hour. On an outdoor barbecue, grill
salmon, skin side down with pesto sauce on top for 15 to 20
minutes or until fish flakes. You can also broil the salmon in
the oven.

Serves: 4
Preparation Time: 1-1/2 hours

RESTAURANT SELECTION

Paillarde of Halibut
in Mint and Southwestern Seasonings

The Phoenician Windows on the Green
6000 E. Camelback Road
Scottsdale

2 baking potatoes
2 T. milk
1 T. unsalted butter
1 bunch green onions, chopped
1/2 bunch cilantro, chopped
salt and ground black pepper to taste
4 (5-oz.) halibut fillets (pounded flat between plastic sheets)
1/2 C. mint, chopped
1/4 C. Lenard's Southwestern Seasoning Blend™
1/4 C. olive oil
4 leaves radicchio
8 leaves lola rosa
8 leaves baby red oak lettuce
8 leaves arugula
16 leaves mache
8 leaves baby red romaine lettuce
1/4 C. balsamic vinegar
1/4 C. mango, pureed
1 T. unsalted butter
1 ear corn taken off of cob and blanched

Procedure: Peel and boil potatoes until soft. Pass through a food mill and add milk, butter, green onions, cilantro, salt and pepper to taste. Coat halibut in chopped mint and then Southwestern Seasoning. Heat a sauté pan with the olive oil in it until very hot.

Add the halibut fillets and cook one minute on each side. Remove halibut from the pan and keep in a warm place. Add lettuces to pan, then add balsamic vinegar. Remove lettuces as they become wilted and place in a ring on the middle of a plate. Let vinegar reduce by half of its original volume. Add mango puree and bring to a boil. Add butter and whisk into sauce slowly. Place amount of mashed potatoes in the center of the ring of wilted lettuces. Spoon the sauce around the lettuces. Place the halibut on top of the mashed potatoes. Heat corn and sprinkle around the plate.

Serves: 4

Chef Lenard R. Rubin

Lemon Grilled Shrimp

One way Arizonans keep their homes cool in the summer is by cooking outside. These shrimp are quick, easy to prepare and delicious.

1/3 C. lemon juice
1 T. vegetable oil
1 tsp. parsley
1/8 tsp. minced garlic powder
1/2 tsp. grated lemon rind
1/2 tsp. dry mustard
pepper to taste
30 lg. shrimp, peeled and deveined
6 wooden skewers

In a large bowl, combine lemon juice, oil, parsley, garlic powder, lemon rind, mustard and pepper. Add shrimp and coat well. Refrigerate for 30 minutes. Remove shrimp from marinade. Set marinade aside. Place shrimp on skewers. Cook over a medium hot grill for 3 minutes on each side. Brush frequently with marinade. Shrimp are done when they turn pink.

Serves: 4 to 6
Preparation Time: 45 minutes

Cal	Pro	Carb	Fat	Chol	Sod	Fib
72	8g	2g	3g	48mg	100mg	0g

Pescado Rojo

Fish with Red Sauce is an enjoyable way to introduce your family to fish.

1 (14-1/2-oz.) can tomatoes, chopped
1 med. onion, chopped
2 cloves garlic, minced
1/4 tsp. ground coriander
2 oz. chopped jalapeño peppers
1/4 C. freshly squeezed lime juice
1 lb. white fish, such as cod, orange roughy or red
        snapper, cut in serving size pieces
1/2 C. green olives, stuffed with pimentos, for garnish

Preheat oven to 400°F. Spray a medium baking dish with vegetable spray. In a large bowl, combine tomatoes, onion, garlic, coriander, peppers and lime juice. Spoon one half of the mixture into the baking dish. Place fish fillets in a single layer over the sauce. Pour remaining sauce over the fish. Bake 20 minutes. Fish will flake when done. Garnish with olives and serve.

Serves: 4
Preparation Time: 30 minutes

Scallops with Catalina Rice

If you're from the coast you'll enjoy this scallop recipe with a Southwestern flair. Sweet and creamy, everybody's going to like it.

2 C. cooked white rice
1 sm. onion, chopped
6 oz. plain low-fat yogurt
1/2 C. mayonnaise (light or fat free)
1/2 C. parsley, chopped
1 T. lemon juice
dash of pepper
12 oz. scallops
1/4 C. bread crumbs
2/3 C. cheddar cheese, grated

Preheat oven to 350°F. Spray an 8" square baking dish with non-stick vegetable spray. In a large bowl, combine all ingredients except bread crumbs and cheese. Spread in baking dish. Sprinkle with bread crumbs. Top with cheese. Bake uncovered 30 minutes.

Serves: 6 to 8
Preparation Time: 1 hour

RESTAURANT SELECTION

Grilled Mexican Shrimp
with Prickly Pear Cactus Fruit Vinaigrette

The Phoenician Windows on the Green
6000 E. Camelback Road
Scottsdale

One of the newest and best known of the Arizona resorts, the Phoenician is located at the base of Camelback Mountain. Windows on the Green offers innovative Southwestern cuisine in a casual setting. Chef Lenard Rubin is known for his unique Southwestern creations, blending unusual ingredients, with traditional elements to produce dishes with distinctive flavors.

30 U-15 shrimp (peeled and deveined)
2 T. chili-garlic paste (available in Oriental markets)
1 bunch cilantro, chopped
juice of 2 limes
1 T. peanut oil
salt and black pepper to taste
6 oz. arugula
1 oz. hearts of palm, sliced
1/2 tsp. balsamic vinegar
1 T. olive oil
1 C. Prickly Pear Cactus Fruit Vinaigrette (recipe follows)

Procedure: Marinate shrimp overnight in the chili-garlic paste, cilantro, lime juice, peanut oil, salt and black pepper.

Grill shrimp until cooked all of the way through (about 3 minutes on each side). While grilling shrimp toss the arugula and hearts of palm with the balsamic vinegar, olive oil, salt and pepper.

Presentation: Place arugula and hearts of palm salad in the middle of the plate. Arrange shrimp around it. Spoon the vinaigrette around the shrimp.

Prickly Pear Cactus Fruit Vinaigrette
2 prickly pear cactus fruit
1/2 banana
2 T. honey
1 T. rice wine vinegar
juice of 1/2 lemon
juice of 1/2 lime

Procedure: Peel skin off of prickly pears and the banana and put fruit into a blender. Add the honey, vinegar, lemon and lime juices and blend until smooth. Season to taste with salt and ground black pepper.

If too sweet for your taste, add more vinegar. If too tart, add more honey. If too thin, add more banana. If too thick, add a dash of apple juice.

Strain through a fine sieve before serving.

Serves: 6

Chef Lenard R. Rubin

Shrimp Verde

This refreshing combination of vegetables and shrimp will have you coming back for more.

1 (13-oz.) can tomatillos, drained
1/4 tsp. cumin
1 Anaheim chile, peeled and seeded
1/4 tsp. Mexican oregano leaves
1 tsp. sugar
1 med. onion, chopped
1 clove garlic, minced
1 tsp. olive oil
1 med. zucchini, sliced 1/4-inch thick
12 oz. shrimp, peeled and deveined
1 (6-oz.) jar of marinated artichoke hearts
2 C. cooked white rice

Puree tomatillos in a food processor. Add cumin, chile, oregano and sugar and mix well. In a medium saucepan, sauté onion and garlic in olive oil until transparent. Add tomatillo mixture. Stir and continue cooking for 3 minutes. Add zucchini. Cook covered for 3 minutes. Add shrimp and artichokes. Cover and cook 3 to 5 minutes. Serve with rice.

Serves: 4
Preparation Time: 20 minutes

Cal	Pro	Carb	Fat	Chol	Sod	Fib
300	25g	32g	8g	119mg	383mg	4g

Stone Springs Salmon Tarts

Even Pacific salmon takes on a Southwestern air when combined with local ingredients.

Filling
8 oz. salmon, cooked and flaked
1/3 C. cream cheese, softened
1 C. cheddar cheese, shredded
1 (4-oz.) can green chiles, diced
3 green onions (scallions), sliced
1/4 tsp. dill weed
1/4 tsp. ground paprika
1/8 tsp. garlic powder
Topping
1/3 C. cracker crumbs
2 T. Parmesan cheese, grated

Dough
2 C. prepared baking mix
1/2 C. water

2 T. butter or margarine, melted

Preheat oven to 400°F. In a large bowl, combine all filling ingredients and mix well. Set aside. In a small bowl, mix together cracker crumbs and Parmesan cheese. Set aside. In a large bowl, combine baking mix and water. Stir until blended. Knead on a lightly floured board for about 1 minute. Roll dough into a 12" X 16" rectangle. Cut into 12 4-inch squares.

In the center of each square place 2-1/2 tablespoons of the salmon mixture and 1/2 tablespoon of cracker mixture. Fold into triangles and crimp the edges with a fork to seal. Brush the tops with butter. Bake 15 minutes.

Serves: 12
Preparation Time: 45 minutes

Zesty Snapper

You'll never call red snapper plain again, once you sample it all dressed up Arizona-style.

1 onion, cut into pieces
2 cloves garlic
2 Anaheim chiles, peeled and seeded
13 oz. tomatillos, drained
1 lb. red snapper
1/3 C. cheddar cheese, grated

Preheat oven to 350°F. Spray a large baking dish with non-stick vegetable spray. In the bowl of a food processor, place onion, garlic, chiles and tomatillos. Process until smooth. Place fish in the bottom of the baking dish. Spread sauce over and sprinkle with grated cheese. Bake for 25 to 30 minutes until fish flakes.

Serves: 4
Preparation Time: 45 minutes

Cal	Pro	Carb	Fat	Chol	Sod	Fib
245	34g	7g	8g	96g	336g	2g

White Fish in Almond and Cilantro

A very pleasant tasting fish dish, but keep your eye on the chiles. Add them slowly and stop before your taste buds begin to sizzle. Serranos are even hotter than jalapeños. For milder tastes switch to Anaheims or canned green chiles.

1 C. chicken broth
1 lb. white fish, such as sole, orange roughy, cod, scrod or
        red snapper
1 T. vegetable oil
2 cloves garlic, minced
3/4 C. French bread, cut into chunks
1/2 C. almonds, slivered
4 chile serranos, canned
1/4 C. fresh cilantro
salt and pepper to taste
1/4 C. shredded coconut

In a large skillet, over high heat, bring broth to a boil. Add fish. Cook 3 to 5 minutes until fish flakes. Remove fish and place in a casserole dish. Set liquid aside.

In a small skillet, sauté garlic and bread chunks in oil.

In a food processor, combine garlic, bread, almonds, chiles, cilantro, salt and pepper to taste and fish liquid. Process until smooth. Pour over fish. Sprinkle with coconut. Place under broiler for 2 to 3 minutes, until coconut is slightly toasted.

Serves: 4
Preparation Time: 15 minutes

POULTRY ENTREES

With America's quest to eat healthy, our menus have fewer red meat dishes. Poultry is low in saturated fat, high in protein and low in calories. In this section, you'll find many ways to prepare chicken and turkey.

Many of the recipes use tortillas. If you have not prepared this type of food before, you will find that they are much more pliable when warmed first. So before beginning to roll an enchilada or fold a burro, we recommend placing the tortilla in a plastic bag and warming it for a few seconds in the microwave. There is no hard and fast rule for how much time it takes to heat a tortilla since the warming time will vary with the number of tortillas and your microwave. But as general rule of thumb, one or two tortillas on high for 20 seconds works well.

Body Sculpture Burritos

Bright Angel Chicken Alfredo

Chicken Fajitas

Chicken Tamale Pie

The Arizona Biltmore Pollo Rellenos

Chicken Yucatan

Cinco de Mayo Chicken

Dynamite Chicken with Vegetables

Exceptional Chicken Enchiladas

Los Abrigados Squab with Cornbread Stuffing

Firestarter Green Chicken

Full Moon Chicken Casserole

Mexican Chicken

Macayo Red Chile Chicken

Monterey Rolled Chicken

Painted Desert Chicken

The Tack Room Oven-Fried Sesame-Cilantro Chicken

Pollo Octubre

Pollo Rancho

Territorial Chicken Stew

Westcourt in the Buttes Mogollon Duck Cognac

Tombstone Chicken

Tumbleweed Chicken

Carefree Turkey Burro

Old Pueblo Turkey Skewers

Stagecoach Tacos

Turkey Enchiladas

Body Sculpture Burritos

When the occasion calls for delicious and low-fat, high protein and high carbohydrates, try this favorite from fitness expert Kent Stevens' collection.

4 boneless, skinless chicken breasts
1/2 tsp. salt-free seasoning powder
1 (15-1/2-oz.) can vegetarian refried beans
8 flour tortillas
1 C. non-fat cottage cheese
2 tomatoes, chopped
1 C. lettuce, shredded

Grill chicken seasoned with seasoning powder on the barbecue for approximately 4 to 5 minutes on each side. Do not overcook. Cut chicken into thin strips. Heat refried beans in microwave for 3 minutes. In a plastic bag, heat tortillas in microwave for 30 seconds.

Place tortilla flat on a plate. Put 2 tablespoons refried beans on tortilla. Then add chicken strips and 2 tablespoons of cottage cheese. Top with tomato and lettuce. Fold sides in and roll up.

Serves: 8
Preparation Time: 20 minutes

Cal	Pro	Carb	Fat	Chol	Sod	Fib
308	24g	38g	6g	41mg	465mg	2g

Bright Angel Chicken Alfredo

Pine nuts and grilled chicken westernize this traditional Italian dish. Variations of this recipe include substituting slivered almonds for pine nuts or shrimp for chicken.

2 tsp. cornstarch
1/4 C. water
1 C. half and half or whole milk
6 oz. spinach, cleaned and trimmed
dash of pepper
4 boneless, skinless chicken breasts (cooked on grill, then
        cut into bite-size pieces)

8 oz. pasta (specialty shape), cooked and drained
1/3 C. pine nuts
dash of paprika

In a small bowl, whisk together cornstarch and water. Set aside. In a large skillet, bring half and half to a simmer, add spinach and pepper. Cook for about 1 minute until spinach wilts, then add chicken and cornstarch mixture. Stir and continue simmering until sauce thickens. Add pasta and pine nuts. Heat through. Sprinkle with paprika

Serves: 4
Preparation Time: 25 minutes

Chicken Fajitas

There are countless ways to make a fajita. Begin here and use your culinary license to assemble your own version. You can add red and green peppers or even switch from chicken to beef or shrimp.

4 boneless, skinless chicken breasts
1/3 C. taco sauce
1 med. onion cut into rings
1/2 T. vegetable oil
6 flour tortillas
1 C. iceberg lettuce, shredded
1 tomato, chopped
1 C. cheddar cheese, grated
6 oz. sour cream, plain low-fat yogurt or guacamole

In a small bowl, marinate chicken in taco sauce. Refrigerate for 4 hours. Remove chicken from marinade and cook on outdoor grill, about 5 minutes per side. Slice chicken in narrow 1-inch long strips. In a small skillet, sauté onions in oil until golden brown.

Place tortillas in a plastic bag and warm in microwave 20 seconds on high. Place tortilla on a plate and fill with chicken, lettuce, tomatoes and onion. Sprinkle with cheese, fold in ends and roll up. Top with sour cream, yogurt or guacamole.

Serves: 6
Preparation Time: 15 minutes

Chicken Tamale Pie

A crustless quiche that's a party pleaser. It's a great carry-along dish for a potluck.

1-1/2 C. chicken, cooked and diced
1 C. corn, canned or frozen
1 (1-1/2-oz.) envelope taco seasoning mix
1 C. cheddar cheese, grated
1-1/4 C. 2% low-fat milk
3/4 C. prepared baking mix
3 eggs

Preheat oven to 400°F. Spray an 8" square baking dish with vegetable spray. Mix together chicken, corn and seasoning mix. Spread into the bottom of the baking dish. Sprinkle with cheese.

In a blender, beat together remaining ingredients until smooth (about 15 seconds on high with a blender). Pour into the baking dish over chicken mixture. Bake 25 to 30 minutes.

Serves: 6 to 8
Preparation Time: 45 minutes

Pollo Rellenos

The Arizona Biltmore
24th Street and East Missouri Avenue
Phoenix

Built in 1929, the architectural influence of Frank Lloyd Wright surrounds the visitor of The Arizona Biltmore. A major renovation project gave the stately resort a face lift in the early 1990s. Enjoy one of their famous, delicious recipes.

Ranchero Sauce (recipe follows)
Spicy Chicken (recipe follows)
1 C. Longhorn cheddar cheese, grated
1 C. Monterey Jack cheese, grated
2 eggs
2 green chiles

Cover bottom of casserole with 1/2 of the Ranchero Sauce. Stuff green chiles with Spicy Chicken, mixed with 1/4 of the Longhorn cheddar and Monterey Jack cheeses. Place on top of Ranchero Sauce, covering with additional sauce and half of the remaining grated cheeses.

Separate egg whites and yolks. Beat egg whites until they form stiff peaks. Beat yolks slightly and gently fold yolks into mixture with remaining cheeses. Spoon mixture over chiles and sauce. Bake in a 350°F oven for 10 to 12 minutes, or until done.

Ranchero Sauce
1/2 C. white onion, diced
1 each--red, yellow and green pepper, diced
2 garlic cloves, chopped
1 each--jalapeño, serrano and yellow wax chile, chopped and seeded
2 T. bacon fat
1/2 tsp. ground cumin
1 tsp. oregano
salt to taste

1 C. chopped plum tomatoes
1 C. tomato puree
1 T. cilantro, chopped

In a heavy saucepan, sauté onion, peppers, garlic and chiles in bacon fat until onions are translucent. Add spices, tomatoes, tomato puree and cilantro. Cook over slow heat for 30 to 45 minutes.

Spicy Chicken
1/2 C. white onion, diced
2 garlic cloves, chopped
1 tsp. ground cumin
1 tsp. black pepper
1 tsp. chili powder
1 tsp. oregano
1 tsp. cayenne pepper
2 tsp. salt
2 T. tomato paste
2 tsp. salad oil
2 qts. water
2 lbs. chicken breast

Sauté onions, garlic, spices and tomato paste in oil for 2 to 3 minutes. Add water and bring to a simmer. Add chicken and bring to a boil. Lower heat and simmer until chicken is tender enough to shred by hand, about 40 minutes. Strain, cool and shred with fingers.

Serves: 2

Executive Chef Peter Hoeffler

Chicken Yucatan

This sweet and sour chicken entrée is destined to become one of your family favorites.

4 boneless, skinless chicken breasts
2 cloves garlic, minced
1 tsp. Mexican oregano leaves
1/2 tsp. cumin
2 T. orange juice
2 T. white vinegar
1/2 T. oil
1 lg. onion, sliced
1 red pepper, seeded and sliced
1 green pepper, seeded and sliced
2 med. tomatoes, chopped
8 corn or flour tortillas

Cut chicken into slices, 1/2-inch thick. Marinate in a mixture of garlic, oregano, cumin, orange juice and vinegar. Allow to set 10 minutes. Drain chicken and set aside. In a large skillet, sauté chicken in oil until the chicken is tender. Add onions and peppers, and stir fry 1 to 2 minutes. Add tomatoes and cook just long enough to heat through. Serve with corn or flour tortillas.

Serves: 4
Preparation Time: 30 minutes

Cal	Pro	Carb	Fat	Chol	Sod	Fib
206	26g	7g	8g	76mg	81mg	1g

Cinco de Mayo Chicken

The red, green and white colors in this dish patriotically recall the colors of the Mexican flag. You can enjoy this one-dish meal on the Cinco de Mayo or any day of the year.

4 boneless, skinless chicken breasts
1/2 T. vegetable oil
1 lg. onion, sliced
1 lg. green pepper, sliced
1 (14-1/2-oz.) can stewed tomatoes
1/2 lb. fresh mushrooms, sliced
1 (4-oz.) can green chiles, diced
6 oz. prepared salsa
2 cups cooked white rice
4 oz. cheddar cheese, grated
1 C. plain low-fat yogurt or sour cream

Cut chicken into 1/2-inch strips. In a large skillet, sauté chicken in oil for 10 minutes, or until chicken is tender. Remove chicken from pan and set aside. In the same skillet sauté onion, pepper, tomatoes and mushrooms for 5 minutes (until vegetables are tender). Add chicken, chiles and salsa to vegetable mixture. Cook 5 minutes. Remove from heat. Serve over rice. Top with cheddar cheese and yogurt.

Serves: 4-6
Preparation Time: 30 minutes

Dynamite Chicken with Vegetables

One of our favorite recipes, this chicken is unlike any you've tasted before. For milder tastes, reduce jalapeños by half or substitute green chiles.

1/2 C. raisins
2 potatoes, cut into 1/2-inch cubes
1 T. garlic, minced
1/2 T. vegetable oil
4 boneless, skinless chicken breasts

Sauce
1 (13-oz.) can tomatillos with liquid
2 med. carrots, grated
1 onion, chopped
1 oz. jalapeño pepper

Topping
1/2 T. vegetable oil
1 C. bread crumbs
1/2 C. pecans

Cover raisins with water to plump. Set aside for 15 minutes. In a saucepan, parboil potatoes for 10 to 15 minutes. Potatoes are ready if tender when pierced with a fork. Drain. In a large skillet, sauté garlic in oil until transparent. Add chicken and sauté until cooked through (about 10 minutes). Remove chicken and set aside.

Puree tomatillos, including liquid, in food processor for 30 seconds, until mixture has a smooth consistency. In the same garlic-laden skillet add tomatillos, potatoes, carrots and onions. Cook over medium heat for 10 minutes. Drain liquid from raisins and add along with jalapeños to vegetable mixture. Simmer for 5 minutes. Return chicken to skillet and heat until warm.

In a small skillet, heat oil. Add bread crumbs and pecans. Sauté until golden brown. On a platter, spread chicken and sauce. Top with bread crumb mixture.

Serves: 4
Preparation Time: 30 minutes

Exceptional Chicken Enchiladas

This is an almost foolproof recipe that'll have your guests howling for more.

1 lg. onion, chopped
2 cloves garlic, minced
1 T. dried cilantro
1 (10-oz.) can enchilada sauce
12 (6-inch) corn or flour tortillas
3 boneless, skinless chicken breasts, cooked and diced
8 oz. cheddar cheese, grated

Preheat oven to 250°F. Spray a large baking dish with non-stick vegetable spray. In a small bowl, combine onion, garlic and cilantro. Pour enchilada sauce onto a plate. Dip one side of the tortilla in enchilada sauce. Lay flat on a smooth surface. Spoon in 1-1/2 tablespoons chicken, 1 tablespoon onion mixture, and 1 tablespoon cheese. Roll up, leaving ends open and place in dish. Repeat until all the tortillas are filled. Spoon remaining sauce on top and sprinkle with cheese. Bake 15 minutes.

Serves: 6 to 8
Preparation Time: 30 minutes

Squab with Cornbread Stuffing
Baked in Sedona Red Rock Clay

Los Abrigados
Canyon Rose
Sedona

Nestled in the Canyon Country of Sedona, Los Abrigados is surrounded by towering red rocks and rich desert landscapes.

2 C. hand-broken cornbread
2 English muffins, hand broken
3 whole eggs
1/4 C. heavy cream
1/2 C. sweetened condensed milk
1/2 C. fine diced, white onion
1/2 C. fine diced, celery
1/2 C. toasted chopped pecans
kosher salt and fresh ground black pepper to taste
1/2 tsp. nutmeg
1/2 tsp. cinnamon
2 T. unsalted butter
2 squab
1/4 C. soy sauce
1 C. spray shortening

Place cornbread, English muffins, eggs, heavy cream, and condensed milk in a bowl. Lightly sauté onion, celery, pecans and spices in butter. Mix all ingredients together. Stuff squab and baste with soy sauce. Wrap squab with parchment paper that has been sprayed with spray shortening. Cover with clay and bake at 300°F degrees for 90 minutes.

Serves: 2

Executive Chef Todd Hall

Firestarter Green Chicken

The name says it all. This one sizzles on your tongue. For a milder version, substitute green chiles for the jalapeños.

Sauce
1 lg. onion, quartered
3 cloves garlic
4 romaine lettuce leaves, cut into pieces
1 (13-oz.) can tomatillos (green tomatoes), undrained
2 oz. jalapeño chiles, drained (or 1 fresh jalapeño, peeled
        and seeded)
4 green onions (scallions), cut in small pieces
1/4 tsp. ground coriander
salt and pepper to taste

6 to 8 boneless, skinless chicken breasts
1 C. low-fat plain yogurt or sour cream

In the bowl of a food processor, combine sauce ingredients. Process to a coarse consistency. Pour into a large skillet and simmer for 20 minutes. Add chicken breasts to green sauce. Simmer another 20 minutes. Remove chicken from pan. Add yogurt to sauce and stir continuously until the mixture is thoroughly combined and heated. Return chicken to sauce mixture and heat for 5 minutes.

Serves: 8
Preparation Time: 1 hour

Cal	Pro	Carb	Fat	Chol	Sod	Fib
196	27g	5g	7g	77mg	154mg	1g

Full Moon Chicken Casserole

Pretty to look at and great to eat. A crunchy combination of bread crumbs and crisp vegetables makes this one-dish meal a real pleaser.

1 egg, beaten
dash of pepper
1 (8-oz.) can cream-style corn
10 oz. frozen broccoli
4 boneless, skinless chicken breasts, cooked and diced
2 T. butter or margarine, melted

116

2 C. herb-seasoned stuffing mix
1-1/2 C. chicken or vegetable broth

Preheat oven to 350°F. Spray a large baking dish with non-stick vegetable spray. In a large bowl, beat egg. Add pepper, corn and broccoli. Spread in bottom of baking dish. Sprinkle chicken on top of vegetable mixture.

In a large bowl, add butter to stuffing mix. Combine until well-coated. Sprinkle over chicken. Pour broth over the stuffing mixture. Bake uncovered 30 minutes.

Serves: 4
Preparation Time: 45 minutes

Mexican Chicken

This version of Mexican Chicken will appeal to food connoisseurs who enjoy the milder flavors of the Southwest.

1 med. onion, chopped
1 clove garlic, minced
1/2 T. vegetable oil
2 sm. tomatoes, chopped
1 green pepper, chopped
1/2 C. catsup
1/4 C. Dijon mustard
2 T. Worcestershire sauce
1/2 tsp. chili powder
1/2 tsp. Mexican oregano leaves
1 chicken, cut up with skin removed
2 C. cooked white rice

Preheat oven to 400°F. In a large skillet, sauté onion and garlic in oil until transparent. Add tomatoes, green pepper, catsup, mustard, Worcestershire sauce, chili powder and oregano. Stir frequently. Continue cooking for 10 minutes. Spray a baking dish with non-stick vegetable spray and place chicken in bottom. Spoon sauce over chicken and bake for 45 to 55 minutes. Serve with cooked rice topped with the remaining sauce.

Serves: 4
Preparation Time: 1 hour

Cal	Pro	Carb	Fat	Chol	Sod	Fib
346	30g	36g	9g	76mg	855mg	1g

RESTAURANT SELECTION

Red Chile Chicken

Macayo Mexican Restaurants
Several locations in the Phoenix area

2 lbs. chicken thighs
1/3 C. vegetable oil
30 oz. boiling water
2 cubes chicken bouillon
2 (10-oz.) cans Macayo Red Chile Sauce™
browned flour*
garlic salt to taste
rice, beans and fresh flour tortillas for serving

* 2 parts all purpose flour to 1 part shortening, heat while stirring in a frying pan until brown color appears.

Lightly fry chicken in oil. Bring water to a boil. Add bouillon cubes. When dissolved add chicken and simmer. When chicken is done, add cans of Macayo Red Chili Sauce.™ Add 4 to 6 tablespoons of browned flour (to desired thickness). Also add garlic salt to taste. Simmer 30 minutes. Serve with rice, beans and fresh flour tortillas.

Serves: 4

Monterey Rolled Chicken

This Kiev-style dish, with a Southwestern twist, can be prepared ahead, refrigerated and baked just 20 minutes before you are ready to serve it.

Sauce
6 oz. prepared salsa
1/4 tsp. cumin
1 tsp. dried cilantro
1/4 C. chopped green onion tops

Breading
1 C. dry bread crumbs
1/2 C. grated Parmesan cheese
1/2 T. chili powder
1 tsp. salt
1/4 tsp. cumin
1/2 tsp. pepper

Filling
4 oz. Monterey Jack cheese
8 boneless, skinless chicken breasts
7 oz. can green chiles, diced

Preheat oven to 400°F. Spray a large baking dish with non-stick vegetable spray. In a small pan, heat sauce ingredients, simmering for about 20 minutes. In a large bowl, combine bread crumbs, Parmesan cheese, chili powder, salt, cumin and pepper. Cut cheese into eight strips.

Flatten chicken. Place a strip of cheese and a tablespoon of green chiles in the center of each piece of chicken. Roll up and tuck the ends under. Roll chicken in dry ingredients and place in the baking dish. Bake uncovered for 20 minutes. Serve chicken topped with sauce.

Serves: 8
Preparation Time: 40 minutes

Painted Desert Chicken

As colorful as the painted desert, this sweet blend of fruit combined with the crunchiness of vegetables is a treat to the eye as well as to the taste buds.

Sauce
2 T. brown sugar
1/3 C. pineapple juice
1/2 C. tomato, peeled and chopped (include juice)
1/4 C. vegetable or chicken broth

4 boneless, skinless chicken breasts
1 med. onion, sliced in rings
2 sm. zucchini, sliced 1/4-inch thick
1 (8-oz.) can unsweetened pineapple rings (reserve juice)
1 C. frozen peas
2 pears, fresh or canned, cut in quarters

Preheat oven to 375°F. In a medium bowl, combine sauce ingredients until blended. Set aside. Spray a large baking dish with non-stick vegetable spray. Place chicken in the baking dish. Layer onions, zucchini, pineapple, peas and pears over chicken. Pour sauce over chicken. Cover with foil, place in oven. Bake 20 minutes. Remove cover and bake another 20 minutes.

Serves: 4
Preparation Time: 1 hour

Cal	Pro	Carb	Fat	Chol	Sod	Fib
307	28g	40g	7g	76mg	402mg	4g

RESTAURANT SELECTION

Oven-Fried Sesame-Cilantro Chicken

The Tack Room
2800 Sabino Canyon Road
Tucson

4 T. soy sauce
4 T. all purpose flour
3 T. sesame seeds
3 T. chopped cilantro (Chinese parsley)
1/2 tsp. salt
4 T. butter or margarine, melted
12 boneless, skinless chicken breasts

Place soy in a shallow dish. On waxed paper, mix flour, sesame seed, cilantro and salt. Coat chicken with soy sauce, then dip flesh side in flour mixture. Arrange top-side up in baking dish. Drizzle melted butter or margarine over chicken. Bake in 400°F oven about 50 minutes until chicken is fork tender. Baste once during cooking period with drippings in bottom of pan.

Serves: 6

Pollo Octubre

Pumpkin seeds add a nutty texture and flavor to this distinctive chicken dish.

Sauce
1 lg. onion
3 cloves garlic
1 (15-oz.) can whole cooked tomatoes
1 Anaheim chile, skinned, seeded and diced
1/2 C. pumpkin seeds
1 T. sugar
1/4 C. chicken broth

6 boneless, skinless chicken breasts
3/4 C. sour cream (or light sour cream)
1 C. prepared bread crumbs

Preheat oven to 375°F. Spray a medium baking dish with non-stick vegetable spray. On a flat plate spread bread crumbs. Coat each piece of chicken with one tablespoon of sour cream (1/2 on front, 1/2 on back), then dredge in bread crumbs and place in baking dish. Bake for 30 minutes. In the bowl of a food processor combine onion, garlic and tomatoes. Blend until smooth. Sauce will have a thick consistency.

Pour sauce mixture into a medium saucepan and bring to a boil. Simmer for 10 minutes to reduce liquid. Add chili, pumpkin seeds, sugar and broth. Simmer for 20 minutes. Pour over cooked chicken and serve.

Serves: 6
Preparation Time: 1 hour and 45 minutes

Pollo Rancho

One of our favorites, we think you'll agree this old fashioned stew is a savory way to increase your fiber intake.

12 chicken drumsticks or thighs, skin removed
3 med. carrots, sliced
1 lg. onion, chopped
2 stalks celery, diced
1/2 T. olive oil
1/2 T. chili powder

1/2 tsp. crushed red pepper
1 C. chicken broth
1 (15-1/2-oz.) can Great Northern beans, rinsed and drained

Cook chicken on outdoor grill 6 to 7 minutes on each side. In a large Dutch oven, sauté carrots, onion and celery in oil for 3 to 5 minutes. Add spices and broth. Return chicken to pan. Bring to a boil. Reduce heat, cover and simmer for 20 minutes. Add beans. Heat through.

Serves: 6
Preparation Time: 45 minutes

Cal	Pro	Carb	Fat	Chol	Sod	Fib
254	24g	26g	6g	50mg	242mg	8g

Territorial Chicken Stew

If your family members turn up their noses at vegetables, this is a clever way to sway opinions.

1 med. onion, sliced in rings
1/2 T. oil
4 boneless, skinless chicken breasts, cubed
1 (15-1/2-oz.) can kidney beans
1 C. corn
1 C. green beans
1 (15-oz.) can tomatoes, chopped with juice
6 oz. pasta, cooked and drained
1/4 tsp. ground sage
4 drops hot sauce

In a large skillet, sauté onion in oil until transparent. Add chicken. Cook until chicken is almost completely done. Add remaining ingredients. Bring to a boil. Simmer 15 minutes.

Serves: 6
Preparation Time: 30 minutes

Cal	Pro	Carb	Fat	Chol	Sod	Fib
291	25g	33g	7g	67mg	57mg	9g

RESTAURANT SELECTION

Mogollon Duck Cognac

Westcourt in the Buttes
Top of the Rock
2000 Westcourt Way
Tempe

The breast of Muscovy Duck is very meaty and flavorful. We use ducks from Grimaud Farms in Linden, California.

3 Muscovy duck breasts, double, boneless
1 qt. Mogollon Marinade (recipe follows)
2 C. Cognac Sauce (recipe follows)

Garnish
1/2 C. candied walnuts
fresh baby vegetables

You may use other duck breasts, but you will need to vary the quantity and the cooking times.

Marinate 24 hours: Marinate the duck in Mogollon Marinade.

Roast 45 minutes: Place the breast on a rack, over a roasting pan, in the oven. Roast at 200°F. Roasting slowly reduces the fattiness of the final dish. Let cool when done.

Sear 8 minutes: In a hot pan on the stovetop, without oil, sear the duck skin side down for 7 minutes. Turn over and sear 1 minute. The meat may darken slightly. Searing is done to seal in the juices.

Roast 5 minutes: Place the breasts in a pie tin. Bake at 400°F until the meat is medium rare, pink and rosy all the way through. Let rest 5 minutes before carving.

Serve: Using a sharp, thin knife, remove the skin. Carve the duck into thin slices on a diagonal, against the grain. Fan the slices out on a warm plate.

Cover with the Cognac Sauce and garnish with 1/2 cup candied walnuts and fresh baby vegetables.

Mogollon Marinade
2 C. soy sauce
2 T. garlic, fresh crushed
2 T. ginger root, fresh chopped
1 C. scotch
1 C. water
1 C. brown sugar
1/2 C. lime juice

Mix well. Yields 1 qt.

Cognac Sauce
1-1/2 tsp. garlic, minced
1-1/2 tsp. shallots, minced
1-1/2 tsp fresh ginger, minced
1/4 C. cognac
1/4 C. triple sec
1/2 C. orange juice
1/8 C. brown sugar
1-1/2 C. demi-glaze
2 T. cornstarch
salt and pepper to taste

Sauté and simmer: Sauté the garlic, shallots, and ginger until the shallots become translucent. Add the triple sec and reduce by half. Add the orange juice and brown sugar and bring to a boil. Add demi-glaze and simmer for 10 minutes. Thicken with cornstarch, and season with salt and pepper. Yields 2 cups.

Serves: 6

Chef Franklin Biggs

Tombstone Chicken

An easy-to-prepare chicken dish, which is enhanced by the crunchy flavors of the pecans.

6 boneless, skinless chicken breasts
1/3 C. lime juice

Sauce
1/4 C. bread crumbs
1 (15-oz.) can tomatoes, with juice
1/2 T. chili powder
1/4 C. chicken broth

1/2 C. whole pecans

Preheat oven to 350°F. In a large bowl, marinate chicken breast in lime juice for at least 20 minutes. In the bowl of a food processor, combine bread crumbs, tomatoes, chili powder and broth. Process until smooth. Spray a large baking dish with non-stick vegetable spray. Place chicken in the baking dish. Cover with sauce. Sprinkle with pecans. Bake for 20 to 30 minutes.

Serves: 6
Preparation Time: 45 minutes

Tumbleweed Chicken

If you take five minutes to start this before leaving for work, dinner can be ready in less than a half an hour. The flavors are best when the chicken can marinate all day.

Marinade
1 T. lemon juice
1 tsp. dried coriander
1/4 tsp. chili powder
1/4 tsp. garlic powder
1/4 tsp. paprika
1/3 C. orange juice

4 boneless, skinless chicken breasts
1 orange, sliced in rings

In a medium bowl, combine marinade ingredients. Add chicken. Cover and refrigerate several hours. Preheat oven to 375°F. Spray a medium baking dish with non-stick vegetable spray. Place chicken in baking dish. Pour remaining marinade over chicken. Bake uncovered for 25 minutes. Garnish with orange slices.

Serves: 4
Preparation Time: 35 minutes

Cal	Pro	Carb	Fat	Chol	Sod	Fib
195	25g	7g	6g	76mg	76mg	1g

Carefree Turkey Burro

Don't pass by the ground turkey, again. Now you have a delicious and nutritious way to prepare it.

1 lg. onion, chopped
2 cloves garlic, minced
1/2 T. olive oil
1 lb. ground turkey
8 oz. frozen corn
3/4 C. prepared salsa
2/3 C. white wine
dash of salt
dash of pepper
8 to 10 (8-inch) flour tortillas
1/2 C. cheddar cheese, grated

In a large skillet, sauté onion and garlic in oil until transparent. Add turkey and cook until meat is brown. Add corn, salsa, wine, salt and pepper and continue cooking until heated through. In a plastic bag, heat tortillas in microwave for 20 seconds on high.

On a plate, lay tortilla flat and fill with about 1/3 cup of turkey mixture. Sprinkle with cheddar cheese. Fold in ends and roll up.

Serves: 4 to 5
Preparation Time: 20 minutes

Per burro

Cal	Pro	Carb	Fat	Chol	Sod	Fib
226	20g	20g	8g	48mg	241mg	1g

Old Pueblo Turkey Skewers

By basting with the apricot sauce you'll add a gentle sweetness to these crispy vegetables. Consider this an alternative to traditional holiday fare.

Sauce
1/2 C. apricot preserves
1 T. butter or margarine
2 T. cider vinegar
1 T. grated fresh lemon peel or 1 tsp. dried lemon peel

1 lb. grilled turkey, cut into 1-inch cubes
1 red pepper cut into large pieces
1 gold or green pepper cut into large pieces
2 ears corn, cooked and cut into 1-inch rounds
8 baby carrots, cooked, but still firm

In a small pan, combine sauce ingredients. Bring to a boil and reduce to simmer. Remove from heat when butter is melted. On wooden skewers arrange turkey meat and vegetables in colorful patterns. With a pastry brush, coat vegetables and meat with basting sauce. Place on a medium high grill. Heat through, basting as you turn about 5 minutes per side.

Serves: 4
Preparation Time: 30 minutes

Cal	Pro	Carb	Fat	Chol	Sod	Fib
403	29g	64g	8g	75mg	138mg	3g

Stagecoach Tacos

Invite your friends over and you have the fixins for a Make-Your-Own Taco Party.

3/4 C. plain low-fat yogurt
1 envelope (1-1/2-oz.) taco seasoning mix
2 tomatoes, diced
2 C. cubed cooked turkey or chicken
12 taco shells
1 green pepper, chopped

2 C. shredded iceberg lettuce
3/4 C. Monterey Jack cheese, grated

Stir together yogurt, seasoning mix, tomatoes and turkey. Cover and refrigerate 30 minutes to blend flavors. Spoon turkey mixture into taco shells and garnish with green pepper, lettuce and cheese.

Serves: 6
Preparation Time: 45 minutes

Turkey Enchiladas

This is a tasty way to use leftover holiday turkey.

Sauce
2 (10-oz.) cans cream of chicken soup
2 C. turkey, cooked and cut in 1/2-inch pieces (about 1 lb.)
1/2 C. sour cream or plain low fat yogurt
1 (4-oz.) can green chiles, diced

2 C. cheddar cheese, grated
1 small onion, chopped
12 (6-inch) corn or flour tortillas

Preheat oven to 350°F. Spray large baking dish with non-stick vegetable spray. In a saucepan, combine sauce ingredients. Heat at medium setting until well-blended and hot. Set aside. In a small bowl, combine cheese and onions. On a flat surface, place an open tortilla. Spoon 2 tablespoons of the cheese mixture into the center. Roll up, leaving ends open and place in the baking dish. Repeat until all the tortillas are filled. Pour turkey sauce over the tortillas and bake for 25 minutes.

Serves: 6 to 8
Preparation Time: 45 minutes

BEEF, PORK, AND OTHER MEAT ENTREES

We've taken a close look at traditional Arizona recipes and searched for ways to lower calories and decrease fat content without compromising the flavors. Overall, these entrées are prepared with a health consciousness that was unavailable to the originators of these delicacies.

From Cowboy Stew to Sweet Country Ribs, you're sure to find a favorite. If you're daring (and can catch one), you might even try the Rawhide Rattler.

Arizona Backyard Burgers

Chimichangas

Carefree Tacos

Rawhide Rattler

Chocolate Enchiladas

Cowboy Stew

Santiago Beef Stew

Show Low Beef and Vegetables

Loew's Ventana Canyon Resort Seared Loin of Venison

Cappraclo with Marinated FrisseTostada Pie

Macayo Green Chile Con Puerco

San Pedro Pork Tamales

Sonoran Pork Chops

Sweet Country Ribs

Sweet and Sour Burros

Westcourt in the Buttes Beef and Veal Medallion Duet

Arizona Backyard Burgers

Try this Southwestern version of a traditional favorite.

1 C. Thick and Chunky Salsa (see recipe on p. 20)
4 grilled hamburgers
4 (10-inch) flour tortillas
1/2 C. cheddar cheese, grated
lettuce, shredded

In a small saucepan, heat salsa. On a serving plate, place the hamburger in the center of the tortilla. Spoon salsa over burgers, sprinkle with 1 tablespoon of cheese and a handful of lettuce. Fold opposite sides over each other to close. Secure with a toothpick if needed.

Serves: 4
Preparation Time: 20 minutes

Chimichangas

If you've enjoyed them when eating out, it may be time to try your own hand at these Arizona favorites. The secret to the chimi is the delicate blend of spices in which the meat is tenderized.

1-1/2 lbs. boneless chuck steak
1 C. water
2 cloves garlic, minced
1 tsp. chili powder
1 T. vinegar
1 tsp. dried Mexican oregano leaves
1/2 tsp. cumin
1/8 tsp. ground black pepper
8 (10-inch) flour tortillas
1 C. vegetable oil for deep frying
2 C. shredded iceberg lettuce
2 C. guacamole
1 C. sour cream
1 C. Thick and Chunky Salsa (see recipe on p. 20)

In a large skillet, place meat, water, garlic, chili powder, vinegar, oregano, cumin and pepper. Bring to a boil. Reduce heat and simmer for 1 hour or until meat is very tender. Place meat on a flat surface, and using two forks, shred meat.

In a plastic bag, microwave the tortillas on high for 40 seconds to soften. Spoon 1/4 cup meat into the tortilla near one edge. Fold edge nearest filling up and over filling--just until the mixture is covered. Fold in the two sides envelope style, then roll up. If needed, use a toothpick to fasten.

In a large skillet, heat 1 cup oil until hot. Place each filled tortilla in the oil and cook until golden brown. Turn and brown the other side. Remove chimi from oil and place on a paper towel to drain. Garnish with shredded lettuce, guacamole, sour cream and salsa.

Serves: 4
Preparation Time: 1 hour and 40 minutes

Carefree Tacos

We've reduced the calories by heating the tortillas in the microwave. For a harder shell, deep fry the tortilla in hot oil, drain on a paper towel and fold in half before assembling.

1 lb. ground beef, lean
1 sm. onion, chopped
1 tsp. chile powder
1/2 tsp. garlic powder
1 (8-oz.) can tomato sauce
10 (6-inch) corn tortillas
1 C. cheddar cheese, grated
2 C. lettuce, shredded
2 tomatoes, chopped
1/2 cup sour cream or plain low-fat yogurt

In a large skillet, brown beef and onion. Drain. Stir in chile powder, garlic powder and tomato sauce. Simmer covered for 10 minutes. Place tortillas in a plastic bag in the microwave for 60 seconds on high. Assemble tacos by layering meat, cheese, lettuce and tomatoes in each shell. Top with sour cream.

Serves: 4 to 6
Preparation Time: 30 minutes

RESTAURANT SELECTION

Rawhide Rattler

Rawhide Steakhouse and Saloon
23023 N. Scottsdale Road
Scottsdale

1 lb. rattlesnake meat
2 whole eggs
1/2 C. milk
1 T. salt
1/2 tsp. white pepper
1/2 tsp. garlic powder
1 tsp. paprika
1 C. all purpose flour
ranch dressing or tartar sauce for dipping

Snake should be cut into filets 2 inches long. Beat eggs into 1/2 cup of milk. Sift salt, pepper, garlic powder and paprika into flour, and put flour into square cake pan. Put snake filets into egg wash making sure each piece is wet. Take snake out of egg wash and place into flour, piece by piece. Make sure each piece is coated evenly, then place on cookie sheet and let batter dry for approximately 10 minutes. Using heavy frying pan with 1 inch of pure vegetable oil, fry snake at 350°F for 2-1/2 to 3 minutes. Serve with ranch dressing or tartar sauce.

Serves: 4 to 6

Chocolate Enchiladas

In the tradition of a Mole Poblano, these enchiladas surprise you with a pleasing combination of cocoa and tomato.

Sauce
1 tsp. chili powder
3/4 C. flour
1/3 C. vegetable oil
1-1/2 C. water
1 C. chicken or vegetable broth
1 (15-oz.) can tomato sauce
2 T. cocoa
1/2 tsp. each garlic powder, onion powder, cumin
1 T. sugar

Filling
1-1/2 lbs. ground beef
1 lg. onion, chopped
1 (4-oz.) can black olives, chopped

15 (6-inch) corn or flour tortillas
16 oz. cheddar cheese, grated

Preheat oven to 350°F. Spray a large baking dish with non-stick vegetable spray. In a large skillet, combine chili powder, flour and oil. Cook over medium heat, gradually adding the water. Use a whisk to blend completely. Add broth, tomato sauce, cocoa, garlic powder, onion powder, cumin and sugar. Simmer 15 minutes.

In a large bowl, mix together ground beef, onion and black olives. On a flat surface, place an open tortilla. Spoon into the center 1/4 cup meat mixture and 1 tablespoon cheese. Roll up, leaving ends open and place in the dish. Repeat until all the tortillas are filled. Spoon sauce on top. Bake 45 minutes.

Serves: 6 to 8
Preparation Time: 1 hour and 15 minutes

Cowboy Stew

This is a favorite old-fashioned stew, with humble ingredients and a distinctive flavor.

1 lg. onion, sliced
1 T. oil
1 lb. beef stew meat, cubed
1 T. flour
2 C. beef broth
2 lg. potatoes, diced
3 lg. carrots, sliced
1 lg. turnip, diced
Even Better with Butter Chile Biscuits (see recipe on p. 152)

In a large skillet, sauté onions in oil until transparent. Remove with a slotted spoon and set aside. Dust beef cubes with flour and brown in oil. As the beef browns, remove from pan and set aside. Pour 1 cup beef broth into the skillet and bring to a boil. Scrape any brown particles that cling to the sides of the pan into the mixture.

Return onions and beef to skillet. Add remaining broth. Reduce heat and simmer for 1 hour. Stir in potatoes, carrots and turnip. Cover again and simmer for an additional 30 minutes. Serve with biscuits.

Serves: 4
Preparation Time: 1 hour and 45 minutes

Santiago Beef Stew

With a tender cut of meat this stew cooks quickly. It can be ready in less than an hour and the best part of all--there's only one pot to clean up!

1 T. vegetable oil
1 lb. London Broil, cut in 1/4-inch slices, across grain
1/4 tsp. ground cumin
1 (15-oz.) can tomatillos, drained
3 med. potatoes, cubed
2 med. zucchini, cubed
1 (12-oz.) jar chili sauce
6 oz. water

In a large skillet, heat oil. Cook meat with cumin until brown. In a small bowl, mash tomatillos with a fork. Add to meat mixture along with potatoes, zucchini, chili sauce and water. Bring to a boil and reduce heat. Simmer covered for 30 minutes.

Serves: 6
Preparation Time: 50 minutes

Show Low Beef and Vegetables

This hearty meat lover's dish is a good source of Vitamin A and fiber.

Sauce
1 C. vegetable or chicken broth
1/3 C. tomato sauce
1 T. Worcestershire sauce
1/2 tsp. garlic powder
dash of pepper

2 lbs. boneless sirloin
2 med. carrots, sliced
1 lg. parsnip, sliced
1 lg. leek, sliced
1/2 head med. green cabbage, shredded
1/2 C. garbanzo beans

Preheat oven to 350°F. In a small bowl, combine sauce ingredients and mix well. Spray a large baking dish with non-stick vegetable spray. Place meat in the bottom of a baking dish. Layer vegetables over meat. Pour sauce over vegetables. Cover and bake for 30 minutes. Remove, cover and bake another 30 minutes.

Serves: 6
Preparation Time: 1-1/2 hours

RESTAURANT SELECTION

Seared Loin of Venison Carpaccio

with Marinated Frisse, Tricolor Bean Salad and Tomato Corn Salad

Loew's Ventana Canyon Resort
7000 North Resort Drive
Tucson

Set in one of Tucson's most scenic areas, visitors come to relax and enjoy great food.

1 lb. venison loin
1/3 C. cooked black beans
1/3 C. cooked blackeye peas
1/3 C. cooked pinto beans
2 tsp. Dijon mustard
3 T. olive oil
1-1/2 T. red wine vinegar
1/4 bunch Italian parsley, chopped
salt and pepper to taste
2 plum tomatoes, diced
2 ears sweet corn
1/4 bunch cilantro
1 tsp. garlic
3 oz. vinaigrette dressing
1 head Italian frisse
3 T. red pepper mayonnaise

Sear venison loin browning well, but keeping mostly raw. Reserve. Combine all beans, Dijon, olive oil, red wine vinegar, Italian parsley, salt, and pepper. Reserve.

Combine plum tomatoes, corn, cilantro (reserving a few leaves for garnish), garlic, salt and pepper. Sauté quickly. Add to 2 oz. vinaigrette. Reserve.

Toss Italian frisse in 1 oz. vinaigrette. To plate: put down 1/4 marinated frisse, then 1/4 of bean mixture. Slice and arrange venison around beans. Sprinkle tomato corn salsa around venison. Put 3 dollops of red pepper mayo on and garnish with cilantro leaves.

Serves: 4

Executive Chef Tony Sindaco

Tostada Pie

This multi-layer dish has a crunchy bottom and a creamy top. Every bite is a mouth-warming delight.

1 lb. lean ground beef
1/2 C. onion, chopped
1 envelope taco seasoning mix
1 (8-oz.) can tomato sauce
1 (16-oz.) can vegetarian refried beans
1 (4-oz.) can green chiles, diced
1/2 C. black olives, sliced
1 C. prepared baking mix
1/2 C. yellow cornmeal
1/2 C. milk
1 egg, beaten
2 T. vegetable oil
1 C. sour cream or plain low-fat yogurt
1 egg
2 C. cheddar cheese, grated

Preheat oven to 375°F. Spray a 9" x 13" baking dish with non-stick vegetable spray. In a large skillet, brown ground beef with onion. Drain. Stir in taco seasoning, tomato sauce, beans, chiles and olives.

In a large bowl, combine baking mix, cornmeal, milk, 1 egg and oil. Beat vigorously for 30 seconds. Spread in the bottom of the baking dish. (Pat with fingers to spread.) Spoon beef mixture over the dough. Mix together sour cream, egg and cheese and spread over the beef mixture. Bake 30 minutes. Let stand 10 minutes before cutting.

Serves: 6
Preparation Time: 50 minutes

Green Chili Con Puerco

Macayo Mexican Restaurants
Several locations in the Phoenix area

When you're ready for a lot of living and great loving, go where Mexican food lovers love to live, Macayo Mexican Restaurants, a family tradition of great Mexican food for more than forty years.

1-1/2 lbs. raw (boneless shoulder) pork meat, diced
4 oz. all purpose flour
4 (4-oz.) cans Macayo Whole Green Chiles™, chopped, 1-inch square
6 oz. white onions, chopped, 1-inch square
1 (14-oz.) can crushed tomatoes
1 tsp. salt
1 tsp. garlic powder
8 oz. water
2 T. lard
1/2 tsp. cumin
1 tsp. chile powder (hot, medium or mild)
1/2 tsp. ground oregano

Brown meat with flour in a large skillet. Add all other ingredients and cook covered for approximately 20 to 30 minutes. Optional ingredient: Add cooked pinto beans.

Serves: 4

San Pedro Pork Tamales

If you're a genuine gringo, you're not supposed to eat the corn husk (don't let anyone convince you otherwise)!
We've made these tamales with ground pork, but if you prefer, you can easily substitute ground chicken or ground turkey.

corn husks from 6 ears of corn
1 lb. ground pork
1 sm. onion, chopped
1/2 C. dry bread crumbs
1 egg
1 T. chili powder
2 T. red wine vinegar
1/2 tsp. garlic powder
1/4 tsp. cumin
1/2 tsp. Mexican oregano leaves
1/8 tsp. dried cilantro

Remove the husks from six ears of corn, discarding silks. Rinse husks and set in a large bowl of water. Soak overnight. In a large bowl, combine all ingredients except the corn husks. Mix well.

Drain and dry husks. Using the widest strips, spread on a flat surface. Fill with 1/4 cup of the meat mixture. Using your hands, spread filling lengthwise across husk. Roll the husk around the meat. If needed, use additional strips of husks to completely cover the meat roll. Tie ends together with a string or a narrow strip of corn husk.

In a steamer basket, or a large pan in which a rack has been inserted to hold tamales 3 inches above the water level, place tamales. Prepare the steamer by filling with 1 inch of water and bringing to a boil. Cover and steam for 15 minutes.

Serves: 5
Preparation Time: 1 hour

Sonoran Pork Chops

Mustard, white wine and orange juice blend for a tangy taste.

2 cloves garlic, minced
1 T. vegetable oil
4 center cut pork chops (1/2-inch thick)
2 tsp. dry mustard
3/4 C. dry white wine
1 C. orange juice
1 med. onion, sliced into rings
1 green pepper, in strips
2 C. cooked white rice

Sauté garlic in oil. Coat pork chops with mustard. Place in skillet with garlic. Brown 5 minutes per side. Add wine, orange juice, onions and green peppers. Simmer 20 minutes.

Serves: 4
Preparation Time: 45 minutes

Sweet Country Ribs

These are an easy oven dish.

1 med. onion, chopped
1 clove garlic, minced
1/4 lb. fresh mushrooms, cleaned and sliced
1 T. olive oil
2 T. red wine vinegar
1 T. honey
1/4 C. lime juice
1 T. prepared Dijon mustard
1/4 C. Worcestershire sauce
1/3 C. water
1/2 C. chili sauce
dash pepper
4 lbs. country-style pork ribs

Preheat oven to 350°F. Sauté onion, garlic and mushrooms in oil until onion is transparent. Add remaining ingredients except ribs. Bring to a boil. Place ribs in a baking dish. Pour sauce over ribs and bake for 1 hour.

Serves: 8
Preparation Time: 1-1/2 hours

Sweet and Sour Burros

If you like it hot, double the amount of cayenne pepper.

1 lb. pork loin, cubed
2 T. vegetable oil
1 med. onion, chopped
2 cloves garlic, minced
1 (7-oz.) can green chiles, diced
1/2 tsp. ground cayenne pepper
1/2 C. chicken broth
3 sm. tomatoes, peeled and chopped
1/4 C. almonds, slivered
2 T. raisins
2 T. red wine vinegar
1/4 tsp. ground cinnamon
1/4 tsp. ground cloves
8 (10-inch) flour tortillas

In a large skillet, brown the pork cubes in oil. Add onion and garlic and sauté until the onion is transparent. Add all the remaining ingredients except the tortillas and heat through.

Place tortillas in a plastic bag and warm in the microwave (about 30 seconds on high). Place tortilla in the center of the serving plate, spoon filling mixture into center and fold in opposite sides. Fold in the remaining two sides and enjoy!

Serves: 4
Preparation Time: 20 minutes

RESTAURANT SELECTION

Beef and Veal Medallion Duet

Westcourt in the Buttes
Top of the Rock
2000 Westcourt Way
Tempe

Wescourt in the Buttes is perched high atop a butte overlooking the Valley of the Sun. The multiple vistas bring inspiration for Southwestern culinary specialties and menu items from around the world. Chef Franklin Biggs is a graduate of La Varenne in Paris. Though this recipe demands a somewhat complicated preparation, the ensuing presentation is worth the work!

2 lbs. beef tenderloin
salt and pepper to taste
2 T. shallots, finely chopped
1 tsp. garlic, finely chopped
1 T. butter
3 lb. spinach, stems removed
pinch of salt
pinch of pepper
2 lbs. veal top round, cut into 6 slices
1 bunch basil, finely chopped (1/8 C. after chopping)
1 bunch fresh tarragon, finely chopped (1/8 C. after
       chopping)
pinch of salt
pinch of pepper
Madeira Glaze (recipe follows)

Sear: Cut the beef into strips 1-inch wide and 3-inches long. Sear lightly on all sides, and season with salt and pepper. Cool.

Sauté: Sauté the shallots and garlic in butter in a skillet over medium heat until the shallots become translucent. Add the spinach and a pinch of salt and pepper. Sauté over high heat until bright green. Cool.

Season: Lightly pound the veal. Season with basil, tarragon, salt and pepper.

Form the rolls: Lay a piece of veal on a sheet of caul fat or butcher twine. Spoon on some spinach mixture, and top with a piece of tenderloin. Roll the veal and spinach around the tenderloin. Encase each roll with caul fat or tie with butcher twine.

Bake 15 minutes: Roast the rolls in a roasting pan at 450°F. Adjust the roasting time for the thickness of the rolls. The chef recommends this dish be served medium rare.

Rest 5 minutes: Remove the rolls from the oven and allow to rest.

Serve: Slice each roll into 3 pieces and serve topped with Madeira Glaze.

Madeira Glaze
2 T. shallots, finely chopped
1 tsp. fresh thyme leaves, without stems
2 C. Madeira
3 C. veal demi-glaze
1 C. Madeira
salt and pepper to taste
arrowroot, as needed

Sauté and simmer 25 to 30 minutes: Sauté the shallots in a skillet until lightly browned. Add the thyme and 2 cups Madeira. Reduce by two thirds. Add the demi-glaze and reduce by half. Add 1 cup Madeira, salt and pepper. Thicken with arrowroot, as needed.

Serves: 6

Chef Franklin Biggs

BREADS AND DESSERTS

From traditional Mexican cornbread to pies, cakes and cookies, there's something for everyone among our selection of breads and desserts. Chocolate lovers will delight in the Brownie Torte and Butterfield Brownies. We've used the Orange Chocolate Squares as a deliciously different birthday treat. There's no pecan pie anywhere that tastes quite like our Southwestern Pecan Pie. We'll let you discover for yourself what makes it so distinctive. So no matter what your heart -- or sweet tooth -- desires, you're sure to find the perfect dessert in these pages.

Ultissimo Mexican Cornbread

Chocolate Angel Squares

Even Better with Butter Chile Biscuits

Corabell's Pantry Cookies

Copper Basin Cookies

The Boulders All-American Toffee Tart

Chocolate Pecan Caramel Cookies

Cowboy Cookies

Happy Jack's Raisin Cakes

Los Abrigados Cornbread Pudding with Nutmeg Cream

Orange Chocolate Squares

Brownie Torte

Mining Camp Applesauce Cake

Butterfield Brownies

Southwestern Pecan Pie

Fresh Rhubarb Pie

Flan

Christopher's Chocolate Tower

The Wigwam Resort's Chocolate Taco

Churros

Sopaipillos

Berry Unbelievable

Ultissimo Mexican Cornbread

We discovered nibblers had attacked this dish while we were waiting for the rest of our meal to cook. This is a moist, almost cake-like bread. Don't expect anyone to eat just one piece.

1/2 C. butter or margarine, softened
1/3 C. vegetable oil
1/2 C. sugar
3 eggs
1/3 C. cheddar cheese, grated
1/3 C. Monterey Jack cheese, grated
1 (14-1/2-oz.) can cream style corn
1 (7-oz.) can green chiles, diced
1 C. flour
1 C. yellow cornmeal
4 tsp. baking powder
1/4 tsp. salt

Preheat oven to 350°F. Spray a 9" x 13" baking dish with non-stick vegetable spray. In a large bowl, combine butter, oil, sugar and eggs. Mix well. Add cheeses, corn and chiles. In a separate bowl, combine flour, cornmeal, baking powder and salt.

Combine wet and dry ingredients. Mix gently until all ingredients are incorporated. Do not overmix. Pour into prepared baking dish. Spread evenly. Bake 45 minutes. Use a toothpick or cake tester to test for doneness. When it comes out clean, remove from oven.

Serves: 16
Preparation Time: 1 hour

Chocolate Angel Squares

This chewy brownie-like dessert can be scooped into a dish and served with ice cream.

1 C. chocolate chips
6 T. butter, melted
3 eggs
1 C. walnuts, chopped
2 C. miniature marshmallows
3/4 C. flour
1/2 C. powdered sugar
1 tsp. vanilla
3/4 C. shredded coconut

Preheat oven to 350°F. Spray an 8" square baking dish with non-stick vegetable spray. In a double boiler, combine chocolate chips and butter. Heat until melted.

Cool, then add in the following order: eggs, walnuts, marshmallows, flour, powdered sugar and vanilla.
Spread in baking dish and bake for 30 minutes. Then sprinkle with coconut and bake an additional 10 minutes. Do not bake more than 40 minutes. Allow to stand 10 minutes before cutting. Yields 16 squares.

Serves: 8
Preparation Time: 45 minutes

Even Better with Butter Chile Biscuits

This light and fluffy biscuit, makes a great accompaniment for a hearty stew.

2 C. flour
1 T. baking powder
1/2 tsp. salt
1/3 C. shortening
2/3 C. milk
1(4-oz.) can green chiles, diced and undrained

Preheat oven to 450°F. Line a large cookie sheet with parchment paper. In a large bowl, combine flour, baking powder and salt. Cut in shortening until well-blended. Add remaining ingredients. On a floured surface, knead dough 12 to 15 times. Roll out to 1/2-inch thickness. Cut into 2-inch rounds with a cookie cutter and place on a cookie sheet. Bake 10 to 12 minutes or until biscuits are golden brown. Yields 20 biscuits.

Serves: 10
Preparation Time: 30 minutes

Corabell's Pantry Cookies

If you've got a package of coconut on hand, these cookies can be made from what's generally found in your cupboard.

1 C. butter or margarine, softened
1 C. brown sugar
1/2 C. sugar
2 eggs
2 tsp. vanilla
2-1/4 C. flour
1 tsp. baking soda
1 tsp. salt
2 C. coconut, shredded

Preheat oven to 350°F. Spray a cookie sheet with non-stick vegetable spray. In a large bowl, cream together butter and sugars. Blend in eggs and vanilla. In another bowl, combine flour, soda and salt. Gradually add to sugar mixture.

Stir in coconut. Drop by teaspoons onto the cookie sheet. Bake 10 to 12 minutes or until tops are golden. Yields 36 cookies.

Serves: 18
Preparation Time: 30 minutes

Copper Basin Cookies

This exceptionally moist oatmeal cookie will have the younguns begging for more.

3/4 C. brown sugar
1/2 C. butter or margarine, softened
1 egg
1 C. applesauce
3 C. rolled oats
1 C. flour
1/2 C. raisins
1 tsp. salt
1/2 tsp. each baking powder, baking soda, cinnamon

Preheat oven to 375°F. Spray a cookie sheet with non-stick vegetable spray. In a large bowl, cream together sugar and butter. Beat in egg. Add applesauce. Stir in remaining ingredients. Drop by teaspoonfuls on the cookie sheet. Bake 12 to 15 minutes or until golden brown.

Serves: 18
Preparation Time: 30 minutes

All-American Toffee Tart

The Boulders
34361 N. Darlington Drive
Carefree

1 recipe Sweet Dough (to follow)
1/2 lb. semi-sweet chocolate, melted
1 recipe Toffee Tart Filling (to follow)
1 recipe Caramel Sauce (to follow)
1 recipe Ganache (to follow)
3 C. whipping cream

Roll Sweet Dough into deep-sided tart pan. Line shell with foil and baking weights. Bake at 375°F until sides and bottom are golden brown. Cool. Paint the sides and bottoms of the shell with melted semi-sweet chocolate. Let sit.

Pour warm Toffee Tart Filling into shell. Bake at 350°F for 45 minutes to 1 hour until set. Chill 4 hours. Remove from tart pan. Pour 1/8-inch thick layer of Ganache on top of set filling. Chill.

Whip 3 C. Cream with 1/2 caramel sauce to stiff peaks. Decorate tart with the whipped caramel cream and chocolate shavings.

Sweet Dough
10 oz. unsalted butter, cold
4 oz. sugar
1 lb. all purpose flour
2 egg yolks
2 T. cream

Cream butter and sugar; add flour and blend. Mix yolks and cream together and add to flour mixture. Mix just until the dough all comes together. Form into a ball and chill several hours.

Caramel Sauce

1 lb. sugar
4 oz. butter
1-3/4 C. cream
juice of 1/2 lemon

Place sugar and lemon juice in a saucepan and start on medium heat, stirring constantly to melt the sugar. After sugar is melted, increase heat to high and continue to stir. Cook sugar until dark brown. Add butter and stir; add cream and stir until smooth. Strain and cool.

Ganache

1/2 lb. semi-sweet chocolate
1/2 lb. bittersweet chocolate
1/2 lb. milk chocolate
1-1/2 C. cream
2 oz. butter

Chop the chocolate and mix all together. Heat cream just to boiling point and pour over chopped chocolate. Stir with whisk; add cubes of butter and continue to stir until smooth. Set aside to cool.

Toffee Tart Filling

1-1/2 C. Caramel Sauce
1-3/4 C. cream
3 egg yolks
2 eggs

Mix all together.

Serves: 8

Executive Pastry Chef Susan Prieskorn

Chocolate Pecan Caramel Cookies

When your sweet tooth calls to you, this irresistible blend of deliciously sweet flavors satisfies.

3/4 lb. caramels, unwrapped
1/4 C. non-fat milk
1-1/2 C. pecans, chopped
1/2 C. butter
3/4 C. brown sugar
1 egg
2 oz. semi-sweet chocolate, melted
2-1/2 C. flour
2 tsp. baking powder
1/2 tsp. baking soda
1 C. sour cream

Preheat oven to 350°F. Spray a cookie sheet with non-stick vegetable spray. In the top of a double boiler, place caramels and milk. Heat until the caramels are completely melted. Turn off heat and add pecans. In the bowl of an electric mixer, cream butter. Beat in brown sugar and egg. Add chocolate. In a large bowl, combine flour, baking powder and soda. Add alternately with sour cream and flour mixture to the batter. Stir in caramel-pecan mixture. Refrigerate 10 minutes. Drop by heaping tablespoons onto the cookie sheet. Bake 12 minutes. Yields 48 cookies.

Serves: 24
Preparation Time: 45 minutes

Cowboy Cookies

You don't have to be riding the range to enjoy cowboy cookies. They're a moist sugar cookie that everyone seems to enjoy.

3 eggs
1-1/2 C. sugar
6 T. orange juice
5 C. flour
2 tsp. vanilla
1 T. baking powder
8 oz. vegetable oil

Combine ingredients and refrigerate overnight. Preheat oven to 375°F. Flour a board. Roll out cookie dough to 1/8-inch thickness and cut with your favorite cookie cutter. Bake for 12 to 15 minutes or until golden brown. Yields 60 cookies.

Serves: 30
Preparation Time: 45 minutes

Happy Jack's Raisin Cakes

Though easy to prepare, this light bar-style cake still receives compliments galore.

1 C. raisins
1 C. water
1/2 C. butter or margarine
1 C. sugar
1 egg
2 C. flour
1 tsp. each baking powder, nutmeg, cinnamon, pumpkin pie
    spice
1/2 tsp. each baking soda, salt
1 C. pecans, chopped

Frosting
3/4 C. powdered sugar
1/4 C. water

Preheat oven to 350°F. Spray a 15" X 10" pan with non-stick vegetable spray. Dust with flour. In a small saucepan, cover raisins with water and bring to a boil. Cook about 5 minutes until raisins begin to plump. Drain raisins, reserving 3/4 cup of the liquid. In a large bowl, cream together butter, sugar and egg. Blend until fluffy.

In another large bowl, combine all dry ingredients, except the nuts. Add alternately with raisin liquid to the creamed mixture. Stir in nuts. Spread in the pan and bake for 20 minutes. Top will be golden brown and cake tester will come out clean. Combine powdered sugar with water for a thin frosting. Spread on cake while still warm. Yields 24 cakes.

Serves: 12
Preparation Time: 35 minutes

RESTAURANT SELECTION

Cornbread Pudding
with Sweet Nutmeg Cream

Los Abrigados
Canyon Rose
Sedona

3 C. heavy cream
1/3 C. cornmeal
1 C. milk, cold
2 eggs
1/2 C. molasses
1/2 C. sugar
1/2 tsp. cinnamon
1 T. fresh ginger, finely chopped
1/2 tsp. salt
4 oz. unsalted butter
Sweet Nutmeg Cream (recipe follows)

Warm the cream 25 minutes at very low heat in a saucepan or double boiler. Combine the cornmeal and milk in a bowl. Add the cornmeal mixture to the cream, stirring constantly. Heat 20 minutes.

Place the eggs, molasses, sugar, cinnamon, ginger and salt in a food processor. Blend until smooth. Stir the puree into the cream mixture. Stir in butter.

Bake 30 minutes at 325°F in glass cookware until firm. Serve warm with Sweet Nutmeg Cream.

Sweet Nutmeg Cream
1 pint whipping cream, whipped
1/2 C. sugar
1 tsp. nutmeg
1 tsp. vanilla

Serves: 4

Pastry Chef Elizabeth Feinberg

Orange Chocolate Squares

A cool, creamy and rich dessert, this is sure to please the chocolate lover. Keep it in mind for special occasions.

8 oz. cream cheese, softened (or light cream cheese)
1-1/2 C. sugar
5 eggs
1/2 C. butter or margarine, softened
2 oz. semi-sweet chocolate squares, melted
1 tsp. vanilla
1/2 C. flour
1/2 C. walnuts, chopped
1 C. mandarin orange slices

Glaze
1/2 C. freshly squeezed orange juice
2 T. cornstarch
2 T. sugar
1/4 tsp. orange peel

Preheat oven to 350°F. Spray a 9" X 13" baking pan with non-stick spray. Line the bottom of the pan with parchment paper. In an electric mixer bowl, blend cream cheese and 1/2 cup sugar until smooth. Add 3 eggs, one at a time and continue beating for 5 minutes. Pour into another bowl and set aside.

In the mixer bowl, beat butter, chocolate, 1 cup sugar and vanilla. Add 2 eggs and beat 2 additional minutes. Add flour and continue beating for 3 minutes. Stir in nuts. Spread chocolate mixture across the bottom of the pan. Pour cheese mixture over chocolate.

Bake 30 minutes or until wooden pick comes out clean. Cool for 10 minutes. Then invert on a wire rack. When cool, remove parchment and turn onto a flat plate with cream cheese side up.

In a small saucepan, place orange juice, cornstarch and sugar and heat on medium high stirring constantly until mixture boils and begins to thicken. Remove from heat. Add orange peel. Spread glaze over cake. Decorate with orange segments. Chill for at least 1 hour (preferably overnight). Cut into squares and serve. Yields 16 squares.

Serves: 16
Preparation Time: 1-1/2 hours

Brownie Torte

This scrumptious chocolate dessert is a brownie, but has the density of flourless chocolate cake, which allows the intensity of the chocolate to surface.

1/2 C. dark corn syrup
1/2 C. butter or margarine
5 oz. semi-sweet chocolate squares
3/4 C. sugar
3 eggs
1 tsp. vanilla
1 C. flour
1 C. walnuts

Chocolate Glaze
3 oz. semi-sweet chocolate squares
1 T. butter
2 T. dark corn syrup
1 tsp. milk

Garnish
1 pt. strawberries, stems removed

Preheat oven to 350°F. Spray an 8" or 9" cake tin with non-stick vegetable spray and line with parchment paper.

In a medium saucepan, bring syrup and butter to a boil, stirring continuously. Remove pan from heat and add chocolate. Stir until melted. Add sugar and incorporate well. Then add eggs, vanilla, flour and nuts. Stir well and pour into prepared cake tin. Bake for 30 minutes. Once cake is cool prepare glaze.

In a small saucepan, melt the chocolate and butter. Remove from heat. Add syrup and milk. Mix well. Pour over cake and spread evenly. Before serving place whole strawberries inverted (points up) around the edge of the torte. Yields 8 brownies.

Serves: 8
Preparation Time: 45 minutes

Applesauce Cake

Mining Camp Restaurant and Trading Post
Apache Junction

East Valley winter visitors have long considered The Mining Camp Restaurant a favorite with its heaping platters of golden brown roasted chicken. The Mining Camp serves family style dinners in the tradition of the early mining camp cook shanty.

1-1/2 C. butter
1-1/2 C. sugar
3 eggs
1-1/2 C. applesauce
1/2 tsp. salt
2 C. flour
2 tsp. baking soda
1 tsp. cinnamon
1/2 tsp. cloves
1/2 tsp. nutmeg
1 C. raisins
1/2 C. walnuts

Cream butter, sugar and eggs until fluffy. Sift dry ingredients. Add raisins and nuts. Add dry mixture alternately with applesauce to butter mixture. Mix thoroughly. Turn into well buttered pan. Bake at 325°F for 1 hour. Keeps well.

Serves: 15

Butterfield Brownies

Take the edge off your chocolate craving with just one of these fudgy brownies.

4 eggs
1-1/2 C. sugar
2 tsp. vanilla
1/2 lb. butter
4 oz. unsweetened chocolate squares
1 C. flour
1 c. walnuts, chopped
1 C. semi-sweet chocolate chips
2 C. miniature marshmallows

Preheat oven to 350°F. Spray a 9" X 11" baking dish with non-stick vegetable spray. Beat eggs until thickened, add sugar gradually and beat well. Add vanilla. Melt butter and chocolate squares together. Add to creamed mixture. Fold in flour, stir in walnuts, chocolate chips and marshmallows. Bake 20 to 25 minutes. Yields 16 brownies.

Serves: 16
Preparation Time: 40 minutes

Southwestern Pecan Pie

You probably think Arizonan's put beans in everything! But if you didn't know they were here, you probably wouldn't even notice them. Tell your guests this pie has a secret ingredient and see if they can identify it. You're sure to get rave reviews with this dessert.

3/4 C. brown sugar, packed
1/2 C. butter or margarine, melted
4 eggs, beaten
3/4 C. dark corn syrup
1/2 tsp. ground cinnamon
1 C. pinto beans, drained and rinsed
3/4 C. pecan halves
9-inch uncooked, prepared pie shell

Preheat oven to 375°F. In the bowl of an electric mixer, blend brown sugar and butter. Add eggs and mix well. Add corn syrup and cinnamon. Stir in beans and pecans. Pour into a prepared pie shell. Bake 30 minutes. Reduce heat to 350°F and bake another 15 minutes or until knife comes out clean.

Serves: 8
Preparation Time. 1 hour

Fresh Rhubarb Pie

From the first pick of the garden, this is a great way to use rhubarb. We've provided a variation for strawberry season.

1 egg
1-1/4 C. sugar
2 T. flour
1/8 tsp. salt
4 C. rhubarb, cut into 1-inch pieces
pastry for a 2-crust pie

Cinnamon Mix
1/4 tsp. cinnamon
3 T. sugar

Preheat oven to 400°F. In a large bowl, beat egg. Add sugar, flour and salt. Beat for about 2 minutes. Add rhubarb, coating well. Pour into a 9" pie shell. Add top crust and flute edges to make a high standing rim. Cut vents and sprinkle top with cinnamon mix. Bake 40 to 50 minutes or until juice begins to bubble through vent and crust is golden brown.

Variation: Use 3-1/2 C. rhubarb and 1 C. sliced strawberries.

Serves: 6 to 8
Preparation time: 1 hour and 20 minutes

Flan

This is a traditional Mexican custard. Once you try making it yourself, you're sure to appreciate it even more when you're dining out.

1 cinnamon stick, broken into pieces
4 whole cloves
2 cardamom seeds, out of the pods
4 whole allspice
2 C. milk
1 tsp. vanilla
1-1/2 T. water
1/2 C. sugar
6 eggs
1/3 C. sugar

Preheat oven to 350°F. In a cheesecloth bag, place cinnamon, cloves, cardamom and allspice. In a large saucepan, combine milk and vanilla. Add cheesecloth filled with spices. Set aside. In a small saucepan, combine water and 1/2 cup sugar. Cook over high heat until mixture boils and turns golden brown. This will take about 2 minutes. Immediately pour into a 9" soufflé dish and swirl across the bottom and halfway up the sides. This hardens as soon as it begins to cool, so work quickly.

In a large bowl, beat eggs. Add 1/3 cup sugar. Heat milk mixture until steaming hot. Remove from heat. Discard spice bag. Slowly pour cooled milk into egg and sugar mixture. Whisk until well-incorporated. Pour into soufflé dish. In a large baking dish, place soufflé dish and fill outer dish with water at least halfway up the sides of the soufflé dish. Bake uncovered for 40 minutes. Chill for several hours. Loosen edges with a knife. Invert onto serving dish.

Serves: 8
Preparation Time: 1 hour and 10 minutes

Chocolate Tower

Christopher's
2398 E. Camelback Road
Phoenix

Christopher's has what Connoisseur *magazine calls "the best food in the Southwest."*

Chocolate Mousse
5-1/2 oz. dark chocolate
3 T. unsalted butter
1/4 C. heavy cream
10 egg whites, room temperature
4 T. superfine sugar
parchment paper
2 oz. dark chocolate, melted
5 oz. white chocolate, melted

Espresso Sauce
1 C. half and half
1/2 vanilla bean
12 espresso beans
4 egg yolks
3-1/2 T. sugar

Garnish
3 T. vanilla sauce
16 slices fresh figs
8 strawberry fans
12 blackberries, halved
2 C. raspberries
8 mint sprigs

For the mousse, slowly melt the dark chocolate and the butter in a double boiler, stirring occasionally to blend. Whip the cream until stiff and set it aside. In a stainless steel mixing bowl, whip the egg whites with the sugar until stiff peaks form.

In a steady stream, fold the melted chocolate and butter mixture into stiff egg whites, scraping the bottom of the bowl until the chocolate is fully incorporated into the whites. Fold the whipped cream into the chocolate egg mixture and keep the mousse well-chilled.

Cut 8 parchment paper strips 3-1/2 inches high and 5 inches wide. Roll the strips into tubes, fastened with tape. Stand them up and fill them, using a pastry bag, with the chocolate mousse. Place them in the freezer for 3 to 4 hours, until frozen and carefully unwrap each one. Cut 8 parchment paper strips 5 inches high and 5 inches wide.

With the melted dark chocolate, drizzle a criss-crossed pattern on these paper strips, allowing the chocolate to set up slightly. Carefully pour the melted white chocolate over the criss-crossed pattern of the dark, but only over a 3-1/2-inch by 5-inch area, which will allow for the basket effect on the top of the chocolate tower. Lay each frozen mousse onto a chocolate-coated strip, and wrap it around the chocolate mousse cylinder while it is still pliable. Refrigerate and remove the paper after 5 minutes. Keep in refrigerator for a minimum of 6 hours to soften the frozen mousse before serving.

For the sauce, bring the half and half, with the vanilla and espresso beans to a simmer. In a stainless steel bowl, mix together the egg yolks and sugar. Temper the egg yolk and sugar mixture by adding 1/4 of the scalded half and half; stir well, pour in the remaining half and half, and cook gently over a double boiler, stirring constantly. When the sauce is thick enough to coat the back of a spoon, strain out the beans and let cool.

To serve, rim the inside edge of each plate with a line of vanilla sauce covered with drops of espresso sauce-bringing the tip of a small knife through each drop to create the heart-shaped pattern. Stand each of the chocolate towers up in the center of the plates and garnish the plates with the fresh figs and berries. Fill the basket top of the towers with raspberries and finish them with a sprig of fresh mint.

Serves: 8

Chef Christopher Gross

Chocolate Taco

Arizona Kitchen
The Wigwam Resort
Litchfield Park

Taco Shell
8 oz. semi-sweet chocolate
1/2 tsp. light corn syrup
1/2 tsp. dark rum

Break up the chocolate into small pieces and place into a mixing bowl. Set atop a double boiler that is simmering. Melt and mix chocolate until smooth over the double boiler until it reaches a temperature of 90°F. Add corn syrup and rum and stir until blended and smooth. Do not overmix.

To form the shell, take a 6" X 6" piece of thin cardboard and cut out a circle 5 inches in diameter. You will then have a cardboard frame to form your taco shell.

When the chocolate is ready, place a piece of wax paper on a cookie sheet then the cardboard frame. Spoon 3 tablespoons of chocolate into the center of the circle. Using the cake spatula, spread the chocolate to fill the circle. Remove the cardboard. Drape the chocolate circle and wax paper over a 1/2-inch dowel and hang in the refrigerator to harden. Make sure the wax paper is against the wood. Keep the taco shell refrigerated until ready to fill and serve.

Chocolate Mousse
8 oz. semi-sweet chocolate
4 oz. heavy cream, warmed to a simmer
4 tsp. coffee-flavored liquor
1 pt. heavy cream, whipped

Break up chocolate into small pieces and place into a mixing bowl along with the heavy cream and chocolate-flavored liquor. Set atop a double boiler that is simmering.

Melt and mix chocolate until smooth. Whip the heavy cream until firm peak consistency. When chocolate mix has cooled, gently fold in the whipped cream. Refrigerate mousse.

Assembly
Taco Shells
1/2 pint of strawberries or raspberries (cleaned and washed)
Chocolate Mousse

Chill the dessert plates. Holding the taco shell in hand, fill with a few berries. Using a pastry bag with a star tip, pipe the mousse into the shell. Place the filled taco shell in the center of the plate and serve.

Serves: 6

Pastry Chef Charles Shapiro

Churros

A favorite at street fairs and with young children, churros have a donut-like texture and an ageless appeal.

oil for deep frying
3-1/2 C. flour
1 T. baking powder
1 tsp. salt
2 C. milk, scalded and cooled
2 eggs
1/2 tsp. vanilla

Cinnamon Mix
1/2 C. sugar
1 tsp. cinnamon

Fill deep fryer with oil and heat to 400°F. In a large bowl, combine flour, baking powder and salt. Add milk, eggs and vanilla and mix well. Pour mixture into a pastry bag which has been fitted with a large tip.

Carefully squeeze 6-inch strips into the hot oil. Use long-handled kitchen tongs to turn and remove from oil when golden brown. Drain on paper towels. While still warm roll in cinnamon mix or in powdered sugar. Yields 24 churros.

Serves: 24
Preparation Time: 45 minutes

Sopaipillos

This classic Mexican dessert has become a favorite with Arizonans.

1 pkg. dry yeast
1/4 C. warm water
4 C. flour
1 tsp. baking powder
1 tsp. sugar
1 T. shortening
1-1/4 C. milk, scalded and cooled
1/2 C. powdered sugar
honey or ice cream for serving

Dissolve yeast in warm water. Set aside. In a large bowl, combine flour, baking powder and sugar. With a pastry blender or a fork, cut in shortening. The mixture will be crumbly. Add prepared yeast and milk and mix well. Knead 15 to 20 times on a floured surface. Let stand for 10 minutes.

Fill deep fryer with oil and heat to 400°F. Roll dough into a 1/4-inch thick rectangle and cut on the diagonal to make 4-inch triangular shapes. Carefully drop triangles into the hot oil. Pastry will puff as it cooks. Cook for about 1-1/2 minutes or until golden brown on both sides. Use long-handled kitchen tongs to turn and remove from oil. Drain on paper towels. While still warm, dust with powdered sugar. Serve warm with honey or ice cream. Yields 24 sopaipillos.

Serves: 24
Preparation Time: 45 minutes

Berry Unbelievable

This light refreshing summer treat can be served as a fruit salad or as a dessert by simply adding a slice of pound cake.

1 pt. fresh raspberries, or 1 (10-oz.) pkg. frozen   raspberries
2 T. sugar
1/2 tsp. cornstarch
1-1/2 tsp. water
1 med. cantaloupe, cut into balls

In the bowl of a food processor, puree berries. Pour through a sieve and press with a wooden spoon to separate seeds and extract juice. Discard seeds. Place berry juice in a small saucepan. Add sugar and blend well. Whisk together cornstarch and water then add to berries.

Heat berry mixture over medium heat until mixture thickens and boils, stirring constantly. Set aside to cool. With a melon baller, cut cantaloupe. When ready to serve pour raspberry mixture over cantaloupe balls.

Serves: 4
Preparation Time: 20 minutes

About the Authors

Dorie F. Pass, a Registered Dietitian with sixteen years of experience, has a B.S. degree in Food and Nutrition. She teaches cooking classes at Kitchen Classics in Phoenix and does nutritional counseling at the Spa at the Camelback Inn in Scottsdale. Dorie also operates Simply Supper, an in-home catering service. In addition, she treats family and friends to special culinary creations. Dorie is the author of *Everybody's Doing It...And Here's How to Quit,* an autobiographical account of her own struggle with, and triumph over, an eating disorder.

Dorothy Tegeler, very at home in her Arizona surroundings, is a writer and researcher whose specialty is Arizona travel and destinations. She has introduced thousands of potential visitors and new residents to her favorite state through her other books, *Retiring in Arizona, Moving to Arizona, Hello Arizona!* and *Destination: Phoenix.*

Together, Dorothy and Dorie have combined their complementary skills to bring you the best of Arizona's cooking. They have spent nearly a year creating, testing, revising and simplifying these recipes. *Arizona Favorite's* is the final result of their best efforts. Both authors reside in Phoenix.

Index